Presidential Power and American Democracy

by PHILIPPA STRUM

Rutgers University, Newark

GOODYEAR PUBLISHING COMPANY, INC.
Pacific Palisades, California

To Sidney

Acknowledgments

Undoubtedly, the people most responsible for the writing of this book are the students who have taken my course in the presidency. Their ability to approach the subject with fresh eyes and to separate insight from cliché has been invaluable to me.

Thanks are also due the *New York Times,* which allowed me to include here its previously published accounts of particular instances of decision-making within the Johnson and Nixon administrations. The articles constitute a step-by-step picture of the policy-making process, and thus they are a rarity.

A number of my colleagues have been good enough to spend their time reading the manuscript and offering beneficial comments and suggestions. I am especially grateful to Dean Norman Samuels and Professor Walter Weiker, both of Rutgers University. Mrs. Marjorie Pritsky typed the various drafts with efficiency and patience, and John D'Anton tracked down endless footnotes without once losing his good humor. I am most appreciative of their assistance.

Finally, my thanks go to my family, which has had to live through yet another writing project. Laura has tried valiantly to understand why her mother insists on pounding a typewriter when she could be playing with blocks. I hope that one day she will know the answer. The greatest burden, however, fell upon my husband, to whom this volume is gratefully and affectionately dedicated.

Contents

Preface

Anyone who goes into a good college course on the American presidency with one of the standard texts will quickly discover that there is a great disparity between what the books say and what the students think about the presidency today. Part of the problem is the tendency of some political scientists to view the presidency as an institution and a problem for analysis; whereas, students see it as merely a mechanism for churning out policies. What the young sense is that much commentary on the presidency relies on outmoded assumptions about the office, and fails to convey any real idea of what presidential activity is all about. Basically, modern political analysis of the presidency has failed in four major ways.

The first of these is the promulgation of the president-as-a-white-knight thesis. College students today do not accept the post-New Deal view of the strong president as an unwavering pillar of virtue. On the contrary, the combination of the war in Indochina and an apparent lack of presidential commitment to social justice has led many of them to scorn the president and seek this virtue in congressional heroes. Almost all of the books written about the presidency in the last 35 years, however, contain the assumption that only a strong president can transform our country into the Good Society of platonic theory. Thus, college students of the presidency are turned off not only by presidents, but also by modern analysts of the presidency. They should be, for events of the last three decades have shown that absolute faith in powerful centralized institutions is sadly misplaced.

The second great failure of most current analysis is insistence on ignoring the inevitability of making value judgments. Most political scientists spend a disproportionate amount of time trying to obscure the fact of the normative nature of political science. Very few textbooks on the presidency say "I believe in a strong presidency because the strong presidents of the last few decades have agreed with my notions of what is politically right," but, that is their clear message. The message is hidden largely because it has become fashionable to ignore the expansive area between value-free analysis and bias. It should be possible to establish a model for the ideal presidency, relying on carefully articulated and sound arguments, and to proceed to evaluate presidents and policies on the basis of the new criteria. Obviously, there will be arguments about which model is the most desirable; but, such an approach would have the dual purpose of acknowledging that political science cannot be value-free, and expressing the underlying assumptions in the author's analysis.

Political scientists are fiercely proud of not being journalists. Among those scholars whose raw material is involved with current events, there is an insistence that there be a perpetual distinction between "journalism" and "political analysis." This is nonsense, as any reader of Tom Wicker or John Osborne or Richard Rovere–to name but a few–must know. The putative difference seems to be limited to a time factor. Journalism follows daily events, whereas political analysis looks at its subject with the insight that only can be gained from a long-term view. Each day's report of the president's activities is not political analysis, but any political analysis that does not take this knowledge into account and put it into a coherent framework is worthless. It is vital to know what the president does day-by-day if one is to comprehend what the presidency means to the American political system year-by-year. Thus the book will utilize the best of American journalism to develop a cogent view of presidential power.

Finally, political scientists have ignored the increasingly important problem of presidential isolation. The problem is not a new one, although it has become more serious since the days of the New Deal, and there seem to be no institutional solutions in sight. This problem is examined in Part II.

This book attempts an analysis which avoids these four major pitfalls. Its theme is a basic one: the need for a balance of powers, particularly where power is highly concentrated. The president has too much unilateral power in certain areas of foreign policy, and the Congress has too much unchecked power over domestic affairs. The book also seeks to update the presidency by utilizing examples drawn almost entirely from the Kennedy, Johnson, and Nixon administrations.

The chapters which follow are not meant to replace standard textbooks; the reader will find no section on the electoral process or the president as Chief of Party or even the president and the students. Knowledge of the basic political process is taken for granted. What follows is some thoughts on the presidency designed primarily to stimulate further discussion. Part I examines various aspects of the relationship between president and Congress in order to show that presidential power and congressional power are different approaches to the process of governing, rather than two separate powers. Part II deals with the particular problems involved in presidential isolation and the president's conception of his role. The conclusion is a sketch of the role the president ought to play and the power he ought to have.

The Appendix includes three articles, reprinted from the *New York Times*, which contain a step-by-step analysis of two major presidential decisions. They appear here to fill a gap because most books on the presidency provide little or no sense of the dynamics of the office. Journalists do much better on this score and the students would do well to note the suggestions for further reading included in the bibliography.

I PRESIDENT AND CONGRESS

1

Presidential Power and Powers

Although a plethora of intelligent political scientists has examined the American presidency, most post-New Deal analysis can be organized into the works of two major figures and the schools of thought which have sprung up around them. They are Clinton Rossiter and Richard Neustadt and they represent differing views of the nature and sources of presidential power.

Rossiter saw the presidency as the sum of a number of constitutional and extraconstitutional roles.[1] He read the Constitution as giving the president the powers of Chief of State, Chief Executive, Chief Diplomat, Commander-in-Chief, and Chief Legislator. Custom, statute, and necessity have added to these the extraconstitutional powers of Chief of Party, Voice of the People, Protector of the Peace, Manager of Prosperity, and Leader of a Coalition of Free Nations. It is the combination of all of these roles, according to Rossiter, that constitutes the power of the presidency, although the personality and ability of each president are also important factors.

Rossiter's view concentrates on functions or roles as the source of power. Neustadt,[2] on the other hand, argues that the president's functions by themselves make him no more than a clerk. Neustadt sees the president as having to persuade other people to do what he wants if he wishes to be more than a clerk, and so for Neustadt the keys to presidential power are the choices that the president makes daily.

If the president chooses unwisely, he can lose power:

> . . . his choices of what he should say and do, and how and when, are his means to conserve and tap the resources of his power. Alternatively, choices are the means by which he dissipates his power.

1

He is aided by three factors in his struggle to maintain power: "the bargaining advantages inherent in his job," "the expectations of . . . other men regarding his ability and will to use the various advantages they think he has," and their "estimates of how his public views him and of how their publics may view them."[4] His "vantage points"[5] in Washington and his reputation can add up to power for the president if he chooses wisely in the ways he attempts to exercise it. Thus Neustadt, unlike Rossiter, does not speak of presidential "powers"; rather, he speaks of presidential "power" which is a dynamic entity constantly in need of renewal and reinforcement.

The discussion between the two schools of thought exists in part because the meaning of the Constitution is deliberately vague. Exactly what the relationship between Congress and the president was meant to be is difficult to ascertain. Along with most constitutional and legislative enactments, the American Constitution was fashioned by a group of men with a variety of disparate notions about the nature of the best possible government. Many of their ideas were held in common; for example, they all seem to have believed that an hereditary monarchy was wrong for America, and instead, some system of representative government had to be established. Their disagreements however, were many. Who ought to elect Congress and the president, what were to be the terms of office of these officials, who should have precisely which powers—all were issues over which the founding fathers argued passionately. The Constitution as it stands represents a series of compromises that were necessary if any document was ever to have been accepted by the coalition of writers. One of the factors that perhaps made compromise possible was the lack of delineation of the office of the president.

Apparently most of the founding fathers had no difficulty in visualizing a Congress. Utilizing both the Lockean notion of a sovereign people delegating some of its inherent powers to a legislature and the idea of John Adams that a bicameral legislature could be made to emobdy the desires of both rich and poor, they sketched the picture of Congress in some detail. They provided for the election of its members and their terms in office, and drew up a lengthy list of its powers. The Congress was to be the heart of the new government.

The office of the president, on the contrary, was left relatively amorphous. There was much discussion about how the president was to be chosen, and those who feared that uninformed masses might be too easily swayed by demagogues were successful in persuading the others to adopt a system of indirect election. The president's term was specified. In order to prevent religious tests from being used to bar anyone from the presidency, his oath of office was included. And then, in a few relatively short paragraphs, his powers were delineated:

Article I
Section 7.. . . Every Bill which shall have passed the House of Representatives and the Senate shall, before it become a Law, be presented

to the President of the United States; If he approves he shall sign it, but if not he shall return it, with his Objections to that House in which it shall have originated, who shall enter the Objections at large on their Journal, and proceed to reconsider it. If after such Reconsideration two thirds of that House shall agree to pass the Bill it shall be sent, together with the Objections, to the other House, by which it shall likewise be reconsidered, and if approved by two thirds of that House, it shall become a Law . . . If any Bill shall not be returned by the President within ten days (Sundays excepted) after it shall have been presented to him, the Same shall be a Law, in like Manner as if he had signed it, unless the Congress by their Adjournment prevent its Return, in which Case it shall not be a Law.

Every Order, Resolution, or Vote to which the Concurrence of the Senate and House of Representatives may be necessary (except on a question of Adjournment) shall be presented to the President of the United States: and before the Same shall take Effect, shall be approved by him, or being disapproved by him, shall be repassed by two thirds of the Senate and House of Representatives, according to the Rules and Limitations prescribed in the Case of a Bill.

Article II

Section 2. The President shall be Commander in Chief of the Army and Navy of the United States, and of the Militia of the several States, when called into the actual Service of the United States; he may require the Opinion in writing, of the principal Officer in each of the executive Departments, upon any subject relating to the Duties of their respective Offices, and he shall have Power to Grant Reprieves and Pardons for Offenses against the United States, except in Cases of Impeachment.

He shall have Power, by and with the Advice and Consent of the Senate, to make Treaties, provided two-thirds of the Senators present concur; and he shall nominate, and by and with the Advice and Consent of the Senate, shall appoint Ambassadors, other public Ministers and Consuls, Judges of the supreme Court, and all other Officers of the United States, whose Appointments are not herein otherwise provided for, and which shall be established by Law: but the Congress may by Law vest the Appointment of such inferior Officers, as they think proper, in the President alone, in the Courts of Law, or in the Heads of Departments.

The President shall have the Power to fill up all Vacancies that may happen during the recess of the Senate by granting Commissions which shall expire at the End of their next Session.

Section 3. He shall from time to time give to the Congress Information of the State of the Union, and recommend to their Consideration such Measures as he shall judge necessary and expedient; he may, on extraordinary Occasions, convene both Houses, or either of them, and in

Cases of Disagreement between them, with Respect to the Time of Adjournment, he may adjourn them to such Time as he shall think proper; he shall receive Ambassadors and other public Ministers; he shall take Care that the Laws be faithfully executed, and shall Commission all the Officers of the United States.

The generality of this section of the Constitution is made apparent by considering the matters that are not discussed. The president is authorized to "require the Opinion ... of the principal Officer in each of the executive Departments," but there is nothing in the Constitution about the establishment of those departments. How many departments would there be? What exactly would be their functions? Would a department's "principal Officer" be a politician, or what we would today call a civil servant? How long would the principal officers hold their jobs? Would the president have the right to fire them? Would they, in sum, serve the president, or the Congress, or themselves, or a combination of all three?

Similarly, the president is charged with the duty of informing the Congress of the state of the Union. Exactly how is the president to go about discovering what the state of the Union is? How detailed will be his recommendations for "such Measures as he shall judge necessary and expedient"? Will he simply say that "something should be done about such-and-such," or will he advocate taking specific action to alleviate specific situations, or will he go even further and draft the laws that he hopes Congress will pass?

A careful reading of the six paragraphs gives no meaningful picture of the scope of the presidency today. The president is now nominated during mammoth political conventions—which themselves follow a number of primaries and meetings of state political organizations. He is elected after a lengthy, expensive, and arduous political campaign. He takes advantage of the glamour of his office in campaigning for other members of his party, and he uses the promise of such campaigning (or the threat of no support) as one way of getting various congressmen to vote the way he wishes on particular bills. And yet, the Constitution does not mention parties or conventions or primaries or public opinion polls or the media—all far more important factors today in the election of the president than the Electoral College.

There is no hint in Article II of a sprawling federal bureaucracy employing two and a half million people. There is no mention of press conferences, executive agreements, summit meetings, cabinet meetings, or throwing out the first baseball each season. And yet, all of these are, or represent, essential elements in the modern presidency.

One of the vital areas given too little consideration in the Constitution is foreign affairs. Many of the founding fathers thought that United States involvement with other countries would be minimal, since the older European governmental systems and their "corruption" were deemed antithetical to the promise of the new republic. The United States was to be a brave new experiment in democratic self-government, hopefully untainted by European failures. Today we discover that much of the president's importance is derived from American involvement in foreign affairs. The Constitutional Convention expected him to be dominant in this area, but the sphere was originally perceived as extremely limited.

It was tacitly acknowledged by most of the delegates in Philadelphia that the first president of the United States would be George Washington. Their great faith in him was evidenced by their electing him president of their Convention, and although his reputation had not yet been encrusted with all the legends that school children learn today, he was renowned for both his military skill and his integrity. Washington, it was understood, would simply have to play it by ear; he was trustworthy, and by dealing with the problems of his office as they arose he would set precedents for those who would follow.

There was another element in the minimal attention paid to the office of the president. A long history of misrule and petty tyranny by the royal governors of the colonies along with the mistrust of the English Crown (encouraged especially by Tom Paine's *Common Sense* as well as by the incompetence of the English kings) had led the delegates to fear the potentialities of executive power. They had little experience with a democratically elected executive, and although there were those who hoped that such an executive might become the focus of the government, there was a more general feeling that the less power the executive had the better, within the framework of the power necessary to carry out his functions. The less power he had, the fewer opportunities he would have to misuse it, and the gaps in the constitutional delineation of his power could be filled in by a watchful Congress.

Thus, because Congress was regarded by many as more intrinsically important to the functioning of the government, because the founding fathers had faith in George Washington, because they had lived through misuse of executive power, and possibly, because no one really knew exactly how the new government would work, the day-to-day duties of the president were left largely unspecified. Article II does not define the presidency, it merely hints at it.

The limited nature of Article II has led to much of the intellectual controversy surrounding the presidency. The twentieth century has seen a succession of very powerful American presidents. Since the Constitution does not disclose the sources of their power, how can one explain this? And to what extent does the great power of the president contradict the original intentions of the Constitution? It is questions like these that were responsible for the analyses of Rossiter and Neustadt. Neustadt's formulation here is infinitely more useful than Rossiter's, although both of them tend to place too much positive value on presidential power without considering the uses to which that power may be put (see chapter 2). Nevertheless, it is possible that Rossiter, by concentrating on the functions of the president, lost sight of the dynamics that are of the essence of presidential power, and Neustadt, by concentrating on those dynamics, lost sight of the role played in them by presidential functions. At any given moment, the president may or may not have actual power, but he certainly has potential power. He possesses such potential because his constitutional and extraconstitutional functions listed by Rossiter mean that, whenever he chooses, the president can set the terms of discussion about any governmental action.

Any analysis of modern presidential power must begin with the president as Chief of State. He is considered the embodiment of the nation and as such, he is ever present and prestigious. No other human being in the United States—and possibly, in the world—gets the kind of media coverage he does. Part of his newsworthiness comes from his other powers, but his role as Chief of State is of immense importance. He cannot travel without the full extent of ceremonial pomp: uniformed bands to greet him, uniformed officers to salute him, photographers to scramble for pictures, aides to check on last-minute details, and crowds to cheer him wherever he goes. No matter how uninteresting they may be as individuals, the members of the president's family are news simply because they share his existence first hand. At any newstand you can see womens' magazines with the president's wife and progeny prominently displayed on their covers next to movie magazines with the president's wife and progeny prominently displayed on *their* covers. Few Washington mementos are more eagerly sought than autographed presidential photographs or the pens the president uses in signing legislation.

This great prestige means that when the president decides to do something, he can usually count on almost all the publicity he desires and on the automatic approval of a large segment of the population. This approval may not be sufficient to persuade the legislature or the bureaucracy to do whatever the president wants it to do, but it can be an important factor in his ultimate success.

The president is also Chief Legislator. In addition to the annual State of the Union message, he regularly sends to Congress a number of other official communications: a budget message, an economic message, etc. Much of what he asks may not be accepted, but his constitutional and statutory obligation to send these messages means that he sets the terms of the arguments. Even more important than the mandated messages that the president transmits to Congress are the drafts of proposed legislation in a wide variety of fields. Together, these constitute his "program," and they take up most of the room on the congressional agenda. When for example, President Nixon proposed a Family Assistance Plan as a means of establishing a limit below which a family's income could not fall, the proposal immediately presented a challenge to Congress: to accept the idea, alter it, or reject it. Although some interest groups sought to go outside the scheme entirely to propose completely different approaches to the problems of poverty, there was very little general public debate along those lines. Argument centered almost entirely around the merits of the president's proposal. This is what is meant by setting the terms of the debate. The first person to submit an idea tends to set the terms, and the president's position as Chief Legislator enables him to submit his approach first more often than not.

The president's greatest advantage, then, is that the conjunction of all his powers puts his ideas into prime focus. One of the extraconstitutional powers that Rossiter might have considered is the president as Chief Cure-All. Whenever something goes wrong in the country—whenever unemployment rises, the stock market drops, the cost of living increases, the balance of payments becomes unfavorable, workers in major industries go on strike, pollution levels of air or water worsen, discontented minorities demonstrate—the country automatically turns to the White House for a reaction, if not a solution. Others may then criticize what he has done; or, if he has chosen to do nothing, the country may look for answers elsewhere; but the choice of seizing the initiative and thus providing the publicity only his interest can generate is always available.* The president will not take the lead unless he has both the desire to do so and the political skill to maneuver an outcome favorable to himself. In any case, most of the advantages are on his side. He will not always win, obviously; there are always other forces in Washington and around the country that will challenge his proposals and exercise whatever power they hold to defeat them. Whether the president should get his way depends, of course, on the content of his proposals and is not at issue here. The point is, by the very nature of his job, the president has the first claim to center stage, and the major question facing him is whether or not he can retain it.

The country expects the president to act during external as well as internal crises. He is the only nationally elected official in the United States (except, of course, the vice-president, who has no independent power), and he is theoretically the only one who has some kind of relation to all Americans. He is our national Answer Man. Should his solutions not be forthcoming, or should they prove to be unsatisfactory, we assume that he is simply not doing his job properly. It does not occur to most of us that the problem may not be in his realm to solve. This can be a liability for him; more frequently, it is an asset.

Other powers he has also give the president the initiative. It is often pointed out that his role as Chief of Party does not give him the kind of power that, for example, the British prime minister has. Unlike the prime minister, the president cannot dissolve Congress if the members of his party refuse to vote as he wishes; and party loyalty among congressmen is a sometime thing. This does not mean that being Chief of Party does him no good. He is not only considered to be the leader of his party nationwide; he is its best-known member. His willingness to campaign for congressional candidates can mean the difference between victory and defeat for them; or, at least, the frantic efforts of candidates to gain his presence at rallies indicates they believe it can be important to them. This is especially true in areas where races are strongly contested. Should the president appear and the congressional candidate win, the congressman is in the

---

*The president's primacy can also be a disadvantage. It may force his involvement in an area he would prefer to avoid entirely. Should his view of his job or of the political realities lead him to eschew involvement, he is likely to be criticized for lack of leadership.

president's debt; he's convinced of the president's popularity in the district. Both factors can be important when a president tries to round up votes for a piece of legislation.

So what we have is a president whose powers (or roles) give him the initiative which, through the careful choice of actions, he can turn to political advantage. There are innumerable limitations on his power, but his powers give him a good many weapons in the fight against those limitations.

This is not to say, however, that the president possesses any powers exclusively. The Constitution may be ambiguous about many things, but it clearly establishes a system of checks and balances. The people who wrote it, afraid of the corrupting influence of absolute power, built into it devices by which each branch could be constantly looking over the others' shoulders. It is usual to say that the Constitution embodies a separation of powers; it is less common to notice that the ideas of separation of powers and checks and balances are paradoxical.

Congress does have the legislative power. It considers and passes the bills that become the laws of the land. The president, however, has the responsibility of signing a bill before it can become a law. This means that he acts as a check on Congress; it also means that he, too, has a certain amount of legislative power. The State of the Union address is designed to enable him to suggest legislation or fields for legislation to the Congress; this is part of the legislative process. Similarly, while the executive power is specifically vested in the president, Congress helps to execute the laws. The Senate must consent to presidential appointments to fill high executive positions, the Congress as a whole appropriates the money for their salaries and staffs, and it is the Congress that exercises an "oversight" function by watching how the bureaucracy performs its job.

The Constitution was written by politicians who understood how political institutions operate in practice, and by lawyers who were less interested in theoretical niceties than in putting together a useful and pragmatic document. "Separation of powers" was a good phrase, but the experienced politicians at Philadelphia recognized that no complete separation was possible. What they separated instead of powers was people. Congress as a body is separated from the executive; the terms of senators and congressmen and the president are different; Congress and the president are elected in different ways; the constituencies of all three are different. Thus, each branch exercises what would seem to be the other's powers, and differences between the branches insure a creative tension designed to make tyranny difficult.

Instead of completely separated powers, the Constitution establishes a bargaining process between president and Congress by giving each the ability to hamper the overall designs of the other. If legislation is to be passed, the Congress must make it palatable for the president, or muster enough votes to override a presidential veto, which is difficult in a governmental system that places a low value on party loyalty. If he wants to see his legislative program enacted, the president must be willing to compromise to ensure the support of congressmen with a wide variety of interests. Because of the disparate concerns of their constituents, congressmen who are with the president on one bill may be against him on another. There is rarely a permanent group of congressmen pledged to enact all of the president's proposals; and so the president is almost invariably forced to work with shifting coalitions of congressmen who join forces on one bill and then go their own ways on the next. We speak of the Democratic or Republican leaders of Congress, but they are less leaders than they are chief persuaders. Even the congressional leaders of the president's own party cannot count on enough members of their party to enact the entire presidential legislative program, so the president must always bargain with individual congressmen.

In the same way, congressmen have legislation that they are anxious to see enacted and that the president is either inclined against or inclined not to fight for. They must bargain with him if they are to have any hope of success. The president can promise a congressman his support in the congressman's next election campaign, or for a federal project for his area or for an alteration desired by the congressman in yet another bill, or federal patronage, minimal enforcement of a law which the congressman believes is affecting his constituents adversely, etc. Congressmen can promise the president their votes on other matters, rapid consideration of legislation the president particularly desires, easy confirmation of a presidential appointee, etc. This kind of horse-trading is the essence of the governmental process, and it is adequately provided for in the Constitution.

The implication is that for all practical purposes, it is irrelevant to argue whether a particular power has been given to the Congress or to the president. Each branch recognizes its dependence on the other and usually foregoes action unless it has at least the tacit consent of the other branch. A recent example of this futile argument is the heated discussion about whether undeclared wars waged by the president are unconstitutional. It is argued on the one hand that the Constitution specifically and deliberately gives Congress the sole power to declare war (Art. II Section 8 para. xi) and that it is vital for this provision to be scrupulously observed if one-man rule is to be avoided. Opponents assert that in a nuclear age it is equally vital for the president as commander-in-chief to be able to respond immediately and flexibly to threats to America's security, as for example, President Kennedy did during the Cuban missile crisis of 1962. It is impossible to go through the lengthy lesiglative process, this argument continues, when action must be taken within a number of hours or even a few days.

This argument is possible only if one assumes that the Constitution gives a monopoly over the war power to one branch. This is clearly erroneous. Congress is entitled to declare war and to raise and regulate the armed forces, but the military commander—the man who actually conducts the war—is the president. The war power is actually divided between the two branches. The Constitution thus necessitates a bargaining process.

Quite deliberately the Constitutional Convention voted to deny the president the power to declare war.[6] The delegates were so determined to prevent the president from beginning a war himself that the original draft of the Constitution which gave Congress the power to "make" war was altered when it was realized that this might be interpreted as giving the president the power to start a war unilaterally.[7] While the president was given the power of commander-in-chief and thus the power to direct the war, the legislature alone has the power to declare war and raise and regulate the armed forces. Alexander Hamilton interpreted the role of commander-in-chief as being no more than that of "first general and admiral of the confederacy."[8]

Even as it carefully reserved the right for Congress to involve the nation in a war, the Convention recognized that there might be instances in which the formal legislative process could not apply. The need to act swiftly to repel enemy attack was not invented in the nuclear age. An additional reason for changing Congress' power to "make" war to that to "declare" war was to indicate the Framers' intention to allow the president to repel attacks against the United States without first checking with Congress.[9] This, however, was intended to be an emergency power, extremely limited in scope.

The early presidents clearly recognized the limitations on their war power. President Adams asked Congress to authorize him to wage the limited "undeclared war" with France of 1798-1800.[10] President Jefferson ordered the navy to take defensive measures to protect American citizens against the Tripolitan pirates, but then turned to Congress for permission to take offensive measures.[11] In 1805, Jefferson decided he had cause to fear that Spain might threaten the Louisiana border she shared with the United States and asked Congress for the authority to use whatever protective force might be necessary. Congress turned him down.[12]

Succeeding presidents occasionally took military action on their own initiative, with Congress either tacitly agreeing or belatedly slapping their wrists. President Polk sent troops to repel what he decided was a Mexican invasion of American territory; President Pierce directed American forces to shell Greytown, Nicaragua. In both instances, Congress later passed declarations expressing its outrage at being ignored.[13] President Lincoln's actions may fall into the category of the domestic insurrection power rather than the war power; in any event, in the 12-week interval between the outbreak of hostilities at Fort Sumter and the special July 1861 session of Congress, Lincoln relied on his powers as commander-in-chief and chief executive to add 41,000 men to the armed forces, issue a call for 40,000 volunteers, spend $2 million dollars of Treasury funds for purposes totally unauthorized by Congress, blockade Southern ports, and suspend the writ of habeas corpus. When Congress finally convened, Lincoln invited the members to ratify his actions. Later, again in his role as commander-in-chief, he issued the Emancipation Proclamation freeing the slaves in rebellious states as a way of eliminating the South's work force and thereby undermining the supplies available to the Confederate Army. There was no doubt about Congress' commitment to the cause of union, even without the acts it passed upholding some of Lincoln's actions and appropriating money for the Union forces, so the question of whether or not he had abused his power in acting unilaterally became a moot one.[14]

In recent years, the war power argument has been raised primarily by those who oppose American involvement in Vietnam. If we examine the history of the Indochina war from the time it became an American war, we can see the bargaining process at work—and we can see what happens when the process is ignored. In August 1964, in the midst of a presidential campaign, there was an exchange of fire between North Vietnamese torpedo boats and United States carrier forces in the Tonkin Gulf. Exactly what happened—who fired first and who was where he had no right to be—may never be determined, although the portions of the secret 1968 Pentagon review of the Indochina war published by the *New York Times* in June 1971 seem to indicate that the attacks were provoked by American and South Vietnamese forces in incidents deliberately kept secret from the American public and the Congress. In any event, asserting that North Vietnamese forces had been guilty of an unprovoked attack on Americans, President Johnson asked Congress for what became the Tonkin Gulf Resolution. It authorized him "to take all necessary measures to repel any armed attack against the forces of the United States and to prevent further aggression." There was some doubt at the time, and much more later, about what the resolution really meant, but it was quickly passed by a Congress inclined to rally around president and flag. Thus the president went to the Congress for permission to take whatever measures became necessary to support American troops. The Tonkin Resolution—a congressional declaration—was later to be cited by the Executive branch as its authority for massive involvement in the war.[15]

By June 1965, and following a series of combat incidents in South Vietnam, 50,000 American troops were stationed there. By the end of that summer, American forces had increased to 170,000 and the United States was conducting regular bombing missions over North Vietnam. The war was to continue to escalate for the next three years. During this time, there was no congressional declaration of war—but there was a great deal of congressional activity amounting to tacit congressional consent to the war. The most significant form of this approval was repeated congressional appropriations for the American war effort. At no time were attempts of any magnitude made to deny the president whatever funds he requested in order to carry on the war. So, throughout growing dissent around the country, anti-war demonstrations, and the beginnings of a serious division within the country about the war, Congress appropriated war funds. If the president was in effect declaring war by sending combat troops to Vietnam, Congress was in effect declaring war by appropriating the funds which paid their way.

This is not to imply that there was no congressional opposition to the war. There was, especially in the Senate, and the much-publicized hearings of Senator

Fulbright's Foreign Relations Committee were simply the best-known manifestation. Nevertheless, the Congress as a whole had given its consent to the Tonkin Resolution; in spite of claims by some congressmen that they hadn't really understood what they were voting for (an astonishing admission from those who fancy themselves statesmen), the president had made the gesture of soliciting their support; and congressional opposition was muted. It certainly was not the Congress that kept Lyndon Johnson from running for reelection in 1968.

In 1964, President Johnson had recognized the need to defer to Congress. This need has been understood by many presidents engaged in international exploits of one kind of another, especially since the Versailles Treaty debacle. President Wilson, in helping to engineer the Treaty and the League of Nations it established, and acting out of a stern sense of right, overlooked such mundane political considerations as soliciting Senate support during the negotiations. His drive for American ratification of the Treaty was defeated in good measure because the Senate had no institutional stake in it.

President Johnson's increased escalation of the war after Tonkin Gulf was taken without prior congressional consent. The Senate was particularly incensed since its members believe that the Constitution gives them a special role in the making of foreign policy. Seeing no reason to hope that President Nixon would not emulate his predecessor's example, the Senate in 1969 passed a National Commitments Resolution which called upon the president not to engage in foreign hostilities without the consent of the Congress. In December 1969, the Senate added an amendment to the pending Defense Appropriations Bill prohibiting the president from using any of the bill's funds to send ground troops to Laos or Thailand. Not only was the Senate suffering from wounded institutional pride; it had decided that it could not trust the president to heed the foreign policy wishes of the Senate unless his hands were tied by specific statutory restrictions.

President Nixon completely ignored President Wilson's lesson when he decided to send American troops into Cambodia without attempting to enlist congressional support either before or immediately after the fact. The result is instructive. Some of the subsequent Senate action can be traced to the enormous public outcry that followed the Cambodian invasion and the student deaths in the subsequent protest at Kent State, some to a Democratic Senate's willingness to embarrass a Republican president, and some to the continuing resentment of the Senate over President Johnson's use of the Tonkin Resolution as a declaration of war. While all of these factors undoubtedly had something to do with the ensuing congressional activity, wounded institutional pride can be seen in the steps promptly taken by the Senate. It voted to abrogate the Tonkin Resolution, adding an amendment to that effect to a bill authorizing the sale of arms to other countries. It added an additional amendment, popularly known as the Cooper-Church Amendment, to that bill.

The Cooper-Church Amendment prohibits the president from spending any funds not specifically authorized to retain American forces in Cambodia, sending military advisers to instruct Cambodian forces, providing air combat support for Cambodian forces, and providing other countries with financial assistance to send their advisers or troops to the aid of the Cambodian government. The Amendment took effect on July 1, 1970, the day that President Nixon had promised would see the last American troops out of Cambodia and was designed to prevent similar invasions. The Senate passed the amendment by the substantial vote of 58 to 37. Then, since the addition of the Cooper-Church Amendment made House passage of the entire bill questionable, the Senate voted to approve a concurrent resolution of the two houses of Congress which would repeal the Tonkin Resolution. (A concurrent resolution must be passed by both houses, but does not require the signature of the president to go into effect.) Thus the House could join in abrogating the Tonkin Resolution even if it chose not to approve the Cooper-Church Amendment.

The Cooper-Church Amendment had been championed by the Senate Foreign Relations Committee, chaired by Senator William Fulbright and a bastion of dovish sentiment. That a dovish amendment was voted out by this committee was hardly surprising. The most shocking senatorial action came in the form of the report accompanying the Armed Services Committee's vote on the $2.5 billion military aid fund for Southeast Asia. The report limited any United States-supported operations in Cambodia to the border areas and to actions directly related to the protection of American troops fighting in Vietnam or to acceleration of the Vietnamization program. It also prohibited the use of the bill's funds to support any foreign armies in actions designed to give the Cambodian government military assistance. The latter provision paralleled one of the aims of the Cooper-Church Amendment. What was significant, however, was its inclusion in an Armed Services Committee report. The committee had become a haven for hawks. Its chairman, Senator John Stennis, is a super-hawk who has insisted that the Congress has no right to limit the power of the commander-in-chief once he has taken military action. Senator Stennis naturally voted against Cooper-Church. He was determined to safeguard congressional prerogatives, however, and could therefore argue that the Congress had the authority to restrict the use of military appropriations in countries where American forces were not already engaged. Significantly, the Senate Armed Services Committee amendment was likely to be ratified by the House. Senator Stennis subsequently (May 1971) introduced legislation designed to curb the power of any president to commit the nation to war without the consent of the Congress, although the proposed bill specifically exempted the situation in Indochina and certain "short term" emergencies.

Even before the Cambodian crisis, the president's inability or unwillingness to deal tactfully with the Congress had become a common matter for discussion in Washington and elsewhere. The president was simply ignoring the bargaining mechanism and the Congress responded as might have been expected. Opposition to the president was concentrated in the Senate, which traditionally sees itself as the senior house of Congress and the one most worthy of presidential respect. The vice-president's vote was necessary to prevent the Senate from denying the president the authority to deploy the antiballistic missiles he felt were essential to mainland defense, two of the president's nominees to the Supreme Court fell short of confirmation (something that had not happened for over 30 years), and the president's veto of a medical facilities appropriations bill was overridden. After Cambodia, the Congress—and particularly, but not solely the Senate-continued to make clear its dissatisfaction with the president and with the role he had assigned to Congress. The proposed Hatfield-McGovern amendment to the military appropriations bill which would have required the withdrawal of all American soldiers from Indochina by the end of 1971 was defeated in the Senate by a vote of 39 to 55. A number of senators who voted against the amendment, however, were firm opponents of the war, and made it clear that they voted as they did only to allow the president to conduct negotiations without being tied to a congressional time table.[16] At the same time, 14 senators, including both the Democratic and the Republican leaders and nine senators who had voted against the Hatfield-McGovern amendment, sent a letter to President Nixon urging him to propose a standstill ceasefire in South Vietnam.[17] The Senate later adopted, by a unanimous voice vote, an amendment forbidding the expenditure of American funds to pay foreign troops fighting in Laos and Cambodia. The House of Representatives voted a 2 billion dollar cut in the Pentagon budget in spite of Secretary of Defense Laird's description of the proposed budget as "rock bottom."[18] Also, the two houses overrode the president's veto of a catch-all appropriations bill for a variety of executive departments and independent agencies, with a large number of Republicans voting against the president, and ended the Ninety-first Congress after giving the president only about one-fifth of his requests.[19] The Hatfield-McGovern amendment was again defeated by the Senate in June 1971. Immediately thereafter, the Senate, by a vote of 55 to 42 passed an amendment designed to withdraw all troops from Indochina within nine months, provided that the North Vietnamese release all American prisoners of war. The amendment passed where Hatfield-McGovern was defeated primarily because the new amendment did not specifically withdraw funds from forces already in the field. The Congress could not force the president to treat it as an equal, but it could do its best to make his life miserable.

One of the problems faced by the Congress when the president engages in an undeclared war is that it is politically dangerous for Congress to deny funds meant to support American troops already fighting on some distant field. The president could then easily blame Congress for the deaths of "our boys over there" if appropriations were cut off. It is far more likely that Congress will remind a recalcitrant president of the bargaining process by denying him other legislation he has requested, such as military appropriations unrelated to the war effort or domestic programs. This is precisely what happened in 1970.

Thus all the powers that the Constitution gives to the president or to

Congress are no more than the authority to do something *with the consent,* tacit or otherwise, of the other branch. To act alone, is to proceed at one's own peril. A president will not usually undertake an important move entirely alone, less out of fear of constitutional limitations than out of his need to protect his bargaining position for the implementation of his entire program. The Constitution doesn't give the war power to the Congress, any more than it gives it to the president, for Congress can decide that it is militarily necessary to stockpile certain kinds of armaments, and if the president decides that they are unnecessary, he can simply leave Congress' decision unenforced. Congress can't pressure the president into a war if the president goes to the people and tells them that on the basis of his highly secret information he has decided that no war is necessary. Aspects of the war power—calling for an army, funding the army, directing the army in the field, etc.—are divided between the two branches, but the overall war power is exercised by the president and the Congress together.

If all of this is true, where does it leave presidential power? If one cannot assume that the Constitution's pronouncement that only the Congress shall declare war means that only the Congress has the war power, can one possibly assume that any of the powers seemingly assigned to the president really belong to him? The answer, of course, is no. The president is "Commander-in-Chief of the Army and Navy of the United States, and of the Militia of the several states, when called into the actual Service of the United States," but Congress can deny him the appropriations necessary to field his army; he can make treaties and appoint officials, but only if the Senate agrees; he can communicate his ideas to the Congress in his State of the Union address, but no one need listen; he can execute the laws, but only with the funds and the personnel that Congress is willing to give him.

As Neustadt has suggested, the president's primary power is his power to persuade. His exposure and prestige in the community at large make him foremost and he can utilize that position as a jumping-off point for persuasion. He must still persuade the people with whom he deals, congressmen, bureaucrats, etc., that it is in their own best interests to do what he wants. On the other hand, where Congress is concerned, persuasion must be a two-way street. If Congress wishes to play a meaningful role within the American government, it must frequently persuade the president to go along with its wishes. In the bargaining process, Congress has numbers but the president has position. It is correct to say that his position is derived from his constitutional and extraconstitutional powers, only if one understands that "his" powers are not his exclusively and that the movement from holding potential power to utilizing actual power depends upon his willingness and ability to take advantage of the bargaining process. The process exists because the Constitution separates not powers but players, with no one branch of the government possessing absolute power to perform exclusively.

2

The Neutrality of Power

Children's fairytales are peopled with characters who are only good or only bad. On a somewhat more advanced level, cowboy and Indian shoot-'em-ups or cops-and-robbers dramas assure their audiences that good and bad are easily identifiable and completely incompatible. Unfortunately, too many recent commentators on the presidency never seem to have gone beyond this stage.

Ever since the New Deal, when President Franklin D. Roosevelt arrived in Washington to begin rescuing a country from the Depression, the majority of political scientists have assumed that presidents are good and Congress is bad. This assumption is all the more extraordinary when one considers that from the Civil War through the Depression, with the exception of the Theodore Roosevelt and Wilson administrations, Congress was routinely considered the body that should and did have the great bulk of power. The current trend in political science to equate powerful presidents with good presidents must be understood in the light of the post-Depression transformation of jobs performed by the president and the Congress and the resulting alteration in the relationship between them.

The twentieth century has seen the United States change from a relatively isolated, low-density rural nation to a high-density urban nation deeply immersed in the affairs of the world. The transition has necessitated changes in the governmental system. Surely the greatest political change of the last 40 years has been the enormous growth of the office of the president and the expansion of the power exercised by the president. In 1900, the federal bureaucracy consisted of about 200,000 people; today, it numbers over 2,500,000 people, who make up over 7 percent of the national work force. Much of this growth is attributable to the proliferation of "alphabet agencies" during the New Deal and the following decades; some of it reflects the natural expansion of existing agencies and the establishment of the Executive Office. The bureaucracy—and, nominally, the president—concerns itself with matters ranging from paving the streets of Washington, D.C. to monitoring the activities of potential revolutionaries in Latin America; from developing sophisticated farming techniques, producing atomic energy, and expanding the American space program, to delivering millions of pieces of mail each day.

The enormous growth in the size and concerns of the federal bureaucracy is an indication of the growth of the president's responsibilities, for, in theory, the bureaucracy is an extension of the president. It is perhaps logical to expect that someone whose duties have grown until they touch upon every aspect of our lives would be given the tools to deal with these responsibilities. However, although the bureaucracy theoretically aids the president; in practice, the bureaucracy is a huge problem for him, for he finds himself constantly struggling to control it. As we shall see, the love-hate relationship between the bureaucracy and Congress also complicates the president's job.

The change in the president's job has necessarily altered his relationship with Congress. Where the post-Civil War period saw dominant Congresses and relatively quiescent presidents, it is taken for granted that post-World War II presidents will be strong and dominant. Congress, however, is not entirely happy with the change.

Since Harry Truman, presidents have been expected to submit to the Congress an annual legislative agenda as well as drafts of specific bills. While this does enable a president to set the terms of the debate, it also puts him in an uncomfortable position. Once he has gone on record as favoring certain legislation, the president is forced to fight for it; and when he is unable to win over a frequently recalcitrant Congress, his prestige necessarily suffers. Thus the role of the president as chief legislator implies a good deal of tension between president and Congress. Urbanization adds to the tension.

Urban areas generally experience the greatest problems. The concentration of millions of people exacerbates and highlights problems which are smaller and more manageable elsewhere, such as transportation; pollution of air, water, and land; crime; welfare, etc. Thus it is primarily (but not solely) urban areas which tend to become dissatisfied with the status quo and seek new solutions. The inability of the business sector to adequately deal with the Depression led the majority of Americans to turn to government for solutions, and the recognition that the problems transcended city and state boundaries, along with the unwillingness of state governments to bother with the problems of the cities, made it inevitable for the people to turn to the federal government for help. Three-quarters of the nation's people live in urban areas, so the nationally elected president must be responsive to those areas.

The fact of exaggerated problems in urban areas helps explain why they are often two party areas; namely, Democrats and Republicans have an equal chance of election. Neither party is likely to solve urban problems successfully within any given time period, and when the people become angry enough about a lack of solutions, they are apt to turn to the candidates of the out-party. Thus congressmen from urban districts are less likely to build up the seniority that is necessary to join the ranks of the powerful congressional committee chairmen. This is not true of congressmen from rural areas, and particularly those from Southern rural areas. There, where fewer problems are regarded as serious enough to require federal government assistance, congressmen are usually assured of relatively long terms in Congress and can acquire the seniority that guarantees power. In 1968, nine out of 16 Senate committee chairmanships were held by Southerners. It is rare for a chairman in either house to be younger than 60; many are in their 70s; some have reached their 80s. Their constituents usually see their interests as antithetical to those served by the president, and the age of the chairmen themselves makes it unlikely that they will be eager to welcome change. In addition, they are unawed by the president's prestige and popularity. They have been in Washington for many years and expect to remain for many more; they see no reason to defer to a relative newcomer in the power structure who will disappear from the Capitol scene long before they will.

In spite of the Supreme Court's decision in *Wesberry* v. *Sanders,* some congressmen continue to represent districts composed of significantly fewer people than those represented by others. Congress allots representatives to each state, but it is the state legislatures which draw the district lines, and the tendency of rural-oriented legislatures is to see that rural areas get more than their share of representation. To the extent that the presidential-congressional tension represents a difference in kinds of constituencies, malapportionment exacerbates the problem.

There is also an institutional component to the conflict between president and Congress. The great question for Congress is: if many ideas and drafts of proposed laws originate with the president and his bureaucracy, what role remains for Congress? Does it exist only to draft legislation in those areas ignored by the president?

Realistically, Congress is much more than a mere adjunct to the presidency. Its functions are derived more from the idea of checks and balances than from separation of powers. It examines proposals, provides the necessary time and apparatus for thorough study, and the opportunity for representatives of various segments of the population to voice their opinions, and generally keeps the president from moving too quickly, or from turning off on a road not sanctioned by the majority of Americans. In addition, a good many proposals originate in Congress rather than in the executive branch, although most of the major ones remain in the background until the president becomes interested in them. The names of men like Webster, Clay, Norris, LaFollette, Wagner, and Fulbright are remembered largely because of their innovative roles in the fashioning of governmental policies, although the average congressman tends to be far less creative.

Individual congressmen or individual committees may be responsible for important pieces of legislation, but it is the president that the public—and the Congress—looks to for a coherent legislative program. This seems to prompt a congressional feeling that Congress too, must demonstrate its importance to the public.

One method by which it maintains its prestige is through investigating. Assuming that Congress is charged with the initiation of legislation, it is logical for it to have the investigatory power—for how else but through investigations can Congress decide what action is necessary? Unfortunately, the investigatory power all too frequently degenerates into busywork, with congressmen investigating for the sake of the prestige and the interesting trips an investigation can enable them to take. The focus of investigations is often the bureaucracy. Calling bureaucrats before congressional committees to explain themselves is a handy way of letting the president know that Congress is alive and not prepared to rubberstamp everything he requests. Thus, investigations do nothing to render the president-Congress relationship more harmonious. Another congressional option is alteration of presidential legislation. It is extraordinarily rare for a proposed draft submitted by the president to emerge from committee hearings and congressional debates with its original wording intact. This is often because the initial draft was flawed or because the pressures of demands by constituents or interest groups necessitated changes, but the alterations seem as often to be so minimal in substance as to raise the suspicion that the Congress simply did not want to pass unamended presidential proposals.

Congressmen are far more amenable to interest group pressure than is the president. This is particularly true of representatives whose districts are small enough to enable only a few industries or unions or whatever to figure importantly in campaign contributions and/or votes. Senators, elected by larger numbers spread over larger areas, may find enough interest groups in their constituencies to be able to balance them off against one another and remain relatively free. The president numbers among his constituents all the members of all interest groups. While this does not render him entirely free of pressure, it does minimize it. Thus he is able to propose legislation, seen by some groups as threatening their prerogatives, with a certain degree of impunity; whereas individual congressmen may find groups so strong within their smaller constituencies that they must defer to their wishes and oppose the president's proposals. Any alteration in the status quo is bound to be opposed by some group. If the opposition groups are sufficiently strong in enough geographical areas to affect enough congressmen, or if they are influential with congressmen who are themselves extremely powerful, or if they made a habit of contributing significant amounts of money to enough congressional campaign chests, the legislation may very well be defeated. The president, of course, has his own weapons, and may be able to put through his legislation, but the fact that Congress is more vulnerable to interest group pressure increases the chances of presidential-congressional conflict.

To summarize: differing presidential and congressional constituencies, the power exercised in Congress by aged and rural-oriented committee chairmen, malapportionment, resentment of the president's prestige and exposure, congressional susceptibility to interest group pressure, and Congress' dissatisfaction with a subordinate role result in both the likelihood that Congress will be the more status quo conscious branch and in a good deal of tension between the president and Congress. Because political scientists have recognized the great need for change in the political structure of the United States to enable it to meet the challenges of the twentieth century, they have tended to view congressmen as a bunch of stick-in-the-muds whose function has been to overrepresent the worst tendencies of their constituents and to prevent dynamic presidents from getting anything accomplished. It will be surprising if this trend is not superseded in the next few years by a countertendency to view the president as the bad guy and congressmen as potential heroes. The new trend is resulting from liberal dissatisfaction with the foreign policies of Presidents Johnson and Nixon, and with their Vietnam policies in particular.

It is clear that the majority of today's college students are dissatisfied with the role the United States has played in Southeast Asia. While a smaller percentage of students has actually been involved in antiwar demonstrations, pollsters have found overwhelming antiwar sentiment on the campuses.[1] For reasons best understood by themselves, pollsters are not as interested in surveying college teachers as they are in surveying college students. Nevertheless, the large numbers of professors involved in organizations aimed at cessation of the war make it clear that faculty sentiment parallels that of the students, even if it is somewhat less explosive. It is these teachers, who will write the books of tomorrow, and their students, some of whom will write the analyses of the day after, who have begun to wonder whether the time has not come to curb presidential power. The earlier liberal assumption that increased presidential power only results in desirable policies no longer remains unchallenged. The focus of antiwar activity within the federal government has been the Congress, with special emphasis on the Senate. This has led a good many students who have grown to political awareness during the Vietnamese debacle, and to whom Roosevelt and Truman are no more than names in history books, to reverse the prior formula and assume that the president is evil and that the new white knights are congressmen. The students' heroes are Robert Kennedy, Eugene McCarthy, George McGovern, William Fulbright, William Proxmire, Mark Hatfield, and other past or present antiwar members of Congress. The failure of President Johnson's much-heralded War on Poverty to win more than a few skirmishes is pointed to as additional evidence that the president is inherently doubledealing and untrustworthy; President Nixon's deplorable attitude toward black Americans and toward most social welfare problems merely reinforces this viewpoint. Student feeling about the inherent wickedness of presidents—and the concomitant impossibility of "good guys" being elected president or remaining alive—has risen to such a point that neither President Johnson nor President

Nixon has been able to visit any of the major college campuses for fear of violence. Unfortunately, a viewpoint that sees the presidency as all bad and increased congressional power as all good would be just as inaccurate as its predecessor.

One of the slogans of the day is "All power to the people." Its implication is that it is better to have power in the hands of the people, than it is to have power in the hands of politicians and their Establishment fellowtravelers, because the Establishment, by definition, misuses power. Although the slogan ignores the ability of the people to misuse power as well as the inevitability of an Establishment of one kind or another, it has the virtue of indicating that power should be in the hands of those who will employ it wisely (for the benefit of the greatest number of people possible). Behind this idea lies another that should be central to the thinking of everyone interested in the political process: the neutrality of power.

Power is neither good nor bad. It can be defined as the ability of one person or group to govern or influence the course of action to be taken by others. Possession of power implies that one person can induce another to do something which the second person might not otherwise do, if left to his own devices. On the political level, power is the participation in the decision making process controlled by political bodies (those groups whose decisions can be backed up with the force of law and legal machinery). Thus, in Washington, someone is considered powerful if he is able to influence the passage or the details of a piece of legislation, or if he can influence the way a law is enforced.

If power is in the hands of someone with whose ideas X agrees, then X is likely to applaud that possession of power. If it is in the hands of someone whose ideas are antithetical to his own, X will condemn it. Thus it is not power itself which is good or bad, but rather the exercise of power which can be judged; and, of course, good and evil exist to some degree in the eye of the beholder. As long as modern presidents fulfilled the expectations of the intellectual community, presidential power was lauded and congressional limitations on the president deplored; now that two presidents have utilized their power to formulate policies with which much of the academic world disagrees, presidential power is in trouble with the intellectuals.

Power is an inevitable aspect of political life. Someone must run the machinery of government; someone must decide priorities. Power may be used wisely or foolishly, but its coloration is derived entirely from its users. Franklin Roosevelt had a great deal of power at the same time that Adolf Hitler had a great deal of power. Obviously, power itself is neutral; the use to which it is put is all. It is therefore a little naive for anyone to advocate presidential power or congressional power in the abstract. What is wanted, but not articulated, is neither presidential power nor congressional power but the wise and beneficial use of power and this is not easy to get.

In trying to decide what the balance of power between the president and Congress should be, we could do worse than return to the men who worked through that sweltering Philadelphia summer of 1787. One of the things they understood, in company with Lord Action, is that power tends to corrupt and absolute power tends to corrupt absolutely. Note the word *tends:* power does not always corrupt, and some virtuous souls can wield great power without being corrupted by it, but the chances are good that power will corrupt. Corruption in this context does not necessarily mean the taking of bribes or the deliberate misuse of power; rather, it signifies the tendency of powerful men to do whatever is necessary to guard and enhance their own power without regard for the people on whose behalf the power is supposedly being exercised. It is easy for a powerful man who is absolutely convinced of the rightness of his vision to delude himself that whatever path he takes to achieve his goal is justified. Once persuaded of the absolute legitimacy of his cause, and equally certain that anyone else with his special knowledge and insight would choose as he has, he may close his mind to all opposition and insist on following his course, come what may.

Perhaps demagoguery is one of the occupational diseases of the political world—although extreme egotists are not confined to the political arena. In order to be elected, a politician must sound as if he knows precisely what he is doing. In convincing their publics of this, perhaps too many politicians also delude themselves. The great panoply of public office does nothing to ameliorate this tendency. Both elected and appointed officials are so frequently treated as figures of great wisdom and glamour that it must be difficult for them to avoid thinking they are as good as their images.

The major problem then would seem to be not how to minimize power, but how to insure that no power is abused—or, to revert to the traditional phrase, how to provide for meaningful checks and balances. The men who wrote the Constitution thought that they were doing precisely that by giving the legislature the powers of the purse and the sword while they gave the executive the suspensive veto. If anything, the suspensive nature of the veto and legislative possession of the powers of purse and sword suggest a dominant legislature and a relatively weak executive—and of course, may very well have been what many of the framers envisioned. But it must be remembered that they were laying the foundations for what they expected to be a government concerned almost completely with domestic affairs in a federal system that gave major control over domestic matters to the states. Today, the balance underlying the Constitution has broken down.

The existing relationship, both in foreign and domestic affairs, will be treated in subsequent chapters. It is necessary at this point, however, to examine the most outstanding recent exercise of presidential power in order to indicate why increased amounts of presidential power are not always to be desired.

President Nixon has followed President Johnson's lead of constantly pointing out that he inherited the Vietnamese War from his predecessors. American involvement in Vietnam dates back to 1954, when the French were defeated at Dienbienphu and it became the Eisenhower-Dulles policy to fill the power vacuum left by the subsequent French withdrawal from South Vietnam. A commitment was gradually made to support the government of Ngo Dinh Diem and to aid the South Vietnamese forces fighting in the civil war; by 1961, 600 American military advisers were stationed in South Vietnam. This force had grown to 16,000 by the time of President Kennedy's death. By 1967, when Lyndon Johnson began to run into real trouble with Congress and the electorate over the Vietnamese issue, the issue was more than ten years old. Under these circumstances, no one could plead that time was of the essence and that the president couldn't take the time to respond to congressional and popular dissatisfaction.

President Johnson was prone to pull out of his back pocket results of the latest public opinion polls whenever he became unhappy about antiwar sentiment. The polls invariably showed that more Americans supported his policy in Vietnam than disapproved of it—or at least, more Americans either supported his policy or assumed that whatever his policy was it had to be the correct one—simply because he was the president and thus knew best. What President Johnson seems not to have realized is that when Americans are asked to respond positively to a presidential policy over a long period of time, a plurality or even a hairline majority in support is not sufficient.[2] The American people were being asked to respond positively to the president's Vietnamese policy: they were expected to surrender their sons, pay a surtax, curtail foreign travel and the purchase of foreignmade goods so as to reduce the balance-of-payments deficit, and live with inflation, all in the name of American involvement in Vietnam. If presidents, with the immense advantage that television gives them, cannot get strong popular endorsement for a policy after that policy has been in existence for a number of years, and after there have been an infinite number of presidential television appearances, then it is more than time to reconsider the policy. It may be that the policy is wise from a strategic standpoint, but unwise in terms of the domestic dissension it causes; it may be that the policy is wrong when viewed from any angle at all. If the policy demands only minimal electorate involvement, e.g., the foreign aid policy, which has never been particularly popular, but which barely impinges on the American consciousness, it can function perfectly well with minimal electorate support. Longterm policies which require positive electorate involvement, however, and which do not inspire the support of substantial majorities, must be bad policies. They are bad because they do not represent the wishes of the soverign electorate. They may be fine tactically, they may be fine morally, but they are bad democratically. If they are good in any absolute sense, the answer to the problem of popular support lies in maximum use of the presidential educative power. If, over a period of time, even the president cannot persuade the electorate to support it, the policy must be revised. Ten years is certainly more than adequate for that kind of education.

This is as true in the domestic arena as it is vis-à-vis foreign policy. Integration is a prime example. When presidents were sufficiently certain of their integration policies to be able to formulate them for the American public and when they indicated their firm intention to stand behind those policies, they managed to achieve a good measure of success. Lyndon Johnson was both educating the electorate and persuading it that what he felt had to be done would be done when he adopted the watchword of the civil rights movemement and said in his 1964 State of the Union address, "We shall overcome." President Johnson was concerned about the passage of what would become the Civil Rights Act of 1964. By convincing the people that the measure was both good and inevitable, he mustered the kind of popular support which could be translated into pressure on congressmen to enact the legislation.

While President Johnson was firm in calling for school integration, his administration was less willing to take concrete action that would result in meaningful integration. It was not until 1967 that the Department of Health, Education and Welfare promulgated deadlines for the integration of all grades by September 1970 and made it clear that federal funds would be cut off from districts refusing to comply. Southern integration began to move at a rapid pace only after the guidelines were announced. The gains in integration cited by the Nixon administration are largely attributable to plans laid and machinery established by local school boards and HEW officials as a result of the Johnson guidelines.

Recent studies indicate that the electorate will support a president when he takes strong action, almost without regard to the substantive nature of that action.[3] What the public clearly wants is to be led, particularly by the president. The lack of a strong popular majority in support of integration of Northern schools, of true equality of economic opportunity for black citizens, of large-scale low-income housing to be built outside the ghetto areas, or open admission policies in the public universities is attributable in good part to the lack of such programs. It is clear that the problems suggested above are more intricate and more difficult to solve than those of equal accommodations, or *de jure* segregation. It is equally apparent that there have been powerful forces brought to bear on recent presidents in order to convince them that their support for these programs would constitute political suicide. It should be remembered, however, that from 1954 to 1964 there were voices insisting that the South would never accept integrated accommodations or even token integration, the government was trying to move too quickly, no government can push people faster than they want to go. In spite of such voices of doom, whenever the government acted firmly to carry out a policy that had clear presidential support, the public managed to gradually accept it. Thus the national absence of broad attempts to end secondclass citizenship in all areas, so many years after the beginning made by *Brown* v. *Board of Education of Topeka,* must be laid in important part on the presidential doorstep.

It would not be necessary for a president to exercise an educative function if he took only steps that were already fully approved by the people. Surely, were he to adopt such a mode of behavior, he would lose the right to be called a leader. The essence of leadership is the formulation of new proposals and solutions and the persuading of the public to accept them. Even when the public is generally agreed about the existence of a problem demanding governmental action—as for example, the pollution problem; it is up to the political leadership to organize specific solutions and convince the electorate that some of them should at least be tried. With his ability to command the airwaves and the headlines, the president must bear a major part of the burden of persuasion. Thus a policy that has been in existence for some time, and which demands positive action or at least acquiescence on the part of the public, and that continues to fall short of real popular support, should be abandoned as too divisive—*assuming that the president has made determined attempts to educate the public on the issue.* It would be foolish to argue that since black equality has been the existing governmental policy since at least the early 1960s and that since it still fails to command strong support within the white population it should be abandoned; for the fact of the matter is that true equality for blacks has never been the policy of an American president in the twentieth century or before. The policy of even the most compassionate has been pacification of black militants and white consciences, not equality.

The difference between the issue of black equality and that of Vietnam, from the point of view of presidential power and the educative function, is that two presidents have adhered to a firm policy which has been given constant and significant media coverage and about which they have spoken to the American people—and they have still failed to convince the substantial majority. Thus it was to be expected that large numbers of Americans would become concerned over President Johnson's decisions to escalate the war in Vietnam and President Nixon's unilateral decision to invade Cambodia.

If time was not of the essence in taking any particular step in Vietnam, the same is certainly true of the decision to extend the war into Cambodia. North Vietnamese and Viet Cong activity in that brutalized little country represented no immediate threat to the safety of the United States, if indeed it represented any long-term threat at all. President Nixon could not convince either Congress or a substantial percentage of the electorate that he had to act unilaterally in formulating his new Cambodia policy. There was more than adequate time for consultation with at least congressional leaders, if the need for secrecy precluded full-scale congressional debate. It is no more than customary for the President to inform, if not consult, such congressional figures as the majority and minority leaders of both houses, the armed services committees, the foreign affairs committees, etc. Such consultation might have altered the Cambodia policy before it went into disastrous effect; certainly, it would have minimized congressional resentment of the president's high-handedness and lessened popular fear that the president was determined to act unilaterally on matters concerning Southeast Asia. Even students who mistrust the entire Establishment differentiated between president and Congress in their post-Cambodia demonstrations. The intensive student lobbying of congressmen and the decision to work for antiwar candidates in the November 1970 congressional election represented a tacit recognition that both congressmen and voters were so appalled at the president's disregard for congressional and popular prerogative that they had become more amenable to antiwar pressure.

The answer to the problem of unilateral presidential power may possibly lie in the time factor. Americans in and out of Congress are sharply aware that they live in a nuclear age when instant decisions may be absolutely vital to national well-being and national existence. They are apparently quite willing for the president to act alone in those situations when immediate decisions are obviously necessary. The threat of nuclear weapons has all but killed the "declared war" concept. The concept is also rendered unusable in a limited war by its implications. Thus, for example, a declaration of war names specific belligerents. All possible measures must be taken to weaken the belligerents' forces; these include an embargo on war supplies. If the United States declared war on North Vietnam, all ships on their way there, including those of the Soviet Union and China, would have to be stopped and searched for war materiel. The possible implications are staggering, for Russia and China would have to respond and the conflict could only escalate. This, however, does not imply that Congress has lost or should lose the power to help determine overall foreign policy. Quick response is but one aspect of foreign policy. If military involvement in an area drags out into weeks and months without the president seeking and receiving both congressional and popular support for the involvement, reliance on the need for a quick response becomes fraudulent and a balanced governmental system is in danger of degenerating into one-man rule.

A situation may force a president into taking quick action and the particular action that he takes may be later condemned by some as incorrect or immoral. This was the case with President Johnson's decision to land American Marines in the Dominican Republic during the short but dramatic civil war there in 1965.[4] The president explained to the American public that he sent in the marines to safeguard the lives of Americans in Santo Domingo; later, he added that part of his reason was to prevent a Communist takeover so close to home (the difference between the justification he used initially and his later defense of his action contributed in good part to the famed Johnson "credibility gap"). The action was condemned by some segments of the public as a manifestation of otherwise disgarded Cold War tactics, a return to the discredited "banana diplomacy" of the nineteenth century, a cavalier snub to the Organization of American States, etc. No one argues against the proposition that *if* the action had any merit it had to be taken quickly and without timedelayed congressional consultation.

Infallibility and perfection cannot be built into political institutions. There is no such thing as a government of laws rather than of men, for no law truly exists until it is interpreted and executed by human beings. Humans are not perfect, and they are not smart enough to build perfection into their political machinery. Just as a computer is only as good as the data fed into it by programmers, so political institutions are only as good as the human beings who create and activate them. Thus there is no guarantee that a president who acts unilaterally only when there is no time for congressional consultation will act wisely. In electing a president, we are electing a fallible human being. We hope that he will be less fallible than others, but we would be deluding ourselves if we expected perfection. All we can do is establish enough checks on his power to make sure that he cannot involve us in any broad undertaking without being able to convince a good number of other people that his proposed course of action is a valid one. Given the state of the world today and the existence of nuclear weapons, we cannot do even that when it comes to military actions which must be taken under the pressures of limited time.

Fortunately, most presidential acts occur in situations which are not time-crises. Most presidents have recognized that in noncrisis situations they must consult with Congress, both because of the constitutional distribution of power between legislature and executive and because of the bargaining process necessary if a presidential legislative program is to have any change of passage. Is there anything that can be done about presidents who do not honor the division of power?

There are some things that Congress can do and has done, but these are mainly after-the-fact. The major weapon Congress has is its power over appropriations. Theoretically, a Congress dissatisfied with a president's unilateral deployment of troops can refuse to vote any further appropriations to keep the troops fighting. As stated before, in practice, however, this can't be done. Cutting off the money that feeds and equips "our boys overseas" would be so politically disastrous an act that Congress is virtually precluded from denying or severely limiting appropriations for undeclared wars already in progress. What Congress can do is vent its anger toward aspects of the military program not involved in the undeclared war. As was discussed above, Vice-President Agnew was forced in 1969 to cast the deciding vote in order to prevent the Senate from denying the president the power to proceed with the construction of antiballistic missile sites and the development and deployment of the missiles. The Senate, generally fed up with President Johnson's Vietnam and other defense policies and apparently convinced that President Nixon was not going to be much different, avenged itself on the ABM. In a similar vein, the Congress can indicate its unhappiness by giving the president a difficult time with his domestic programs. President Johnson was able to wring out of Congress virtually no important domestic legislation from 1966 through 1968, when congressional criticism of his Vietnam policy and congressional resentment at his disregard of that criticism were mounting. Part of the limited output can be traced to the natural reaction that was bound to set in after the great accomplishments of the Eighty-eighth and Eighty-ninth Congresses, but an equally important part is attributable to the strained relations between president and Congress that were an aspect of the Vietnam era.

Congress can make life extremely unpleasant for a president who has engaged the country in an undeclared war that Congress doesn't like, but there hasn't seemed to be much that Congress could do to get the country out of the war. Perhaps—and this relates directly to the isolation of the presidency discussed later—one thing Congress can do in the future is to prevent the president from carrying on an undeclared war for more than a limited period of time without making himself available to members of Congress. Thus, for example, Congress could easily append an amendment to all military appropriations bills denying the president the power to deploy American troops in foreign countries where they are not already deployed, or in numbers beyond those already deployed at the time of the passage of the bill, for more than X number of weeks without consulting with the entire membership of certain specified committees; e.g. the armed services and foreign affairs committees of both Senate and House. The difficulty here could lie in the jealousy of the Senate, which might be reluctant to share with House committees what it has often seen as its exclusive interest in foreign affairs (based on the constitutional requirement of the Senate to advise and consent to the making of treaties and the appointment of ambassadors). The insistence that only one house has a valid interest in foreign affairs is ridiculous, both because the House has always had equal power over the appropriations necessary to the conduct of foreign affairs and because foreign affairs today are so inextricably interwoven with domestic affairs that it is impossible to deal intelligently with the one without impinging upon the other. Perhaps the Senate could be persuaded to lay aside its institutional pride in the name of greater congressional power. Mandated presidential conferences with congressional committees and leaders could act as forceful reminders to him that long-term unilateral action on his part destroys the bargaining process vital to the proper functioning of the federal government and raises the threat of defeat of much of his legislative program. If the president has been relatively cut off from popular criticism, such meetings might serve to put him in closer touch with popular opinion. Members of the House of Representatives, especially, concerned about their frequent reelection campaigns, will be anxious to acquaint the president with antiwar sentiment that might damage their own chances of retaining office.

There might well be dangers in this suggestion. Congress, as was mentioned before, is as a body much slower to change than is the presidency. It is slower to agree to changes in policies and it is slower to see the need to change ideology. Congress, for example, persisted in its fondness for the saber-rattling ideology of the Cold War long after the White House had adopted the stance of coexistence. Mandated meetings might therefore limit the flexibility the president needs in responding to international crises. Arthur Schlesinger suggests this possibility in his account of John Kennedy's presidency.[5] At the beginning of the 1962 Cuban missile crisis, Kennedy consulted only with carefully selected advisers. When, with their help, he had decided on a course of action, he called in congressional leaders to inform them of his decision. His comment after the briefing session was, "The trouble is that, when you get a group of senators together, they are always dominated by the man who takes the boldest and strongest line."[6] It should be noted, however, that a statutory requirement to "consult" with congressmen is not quite the same thing as a requirement to seek their consent. It doesn't bind the president to accept congressional advice, but rather guarantees that his door will be open to congressmen and that congressional criticism will be heard. If President Kennedy was correct and senators in their collective capacity do tend to be hardliners, mandated meetings might result in another problem: the president graphically reminded of the bargaining process, might feel himself constrained to take increasingly forceful positions towards international opponents in order to maintain his relationship with Congress. Both of these undesirable possibilities do exist. Nevertheless, it is difficult to believe that such a system could result in any situation vis-à-vis undeclared wars that would be worse than the present one.[7]

To summarize: the American presence in Vietnam and Cambodia should lead even the most diehard proponents of increased presidential power to question their assumption that expansion of power is always a good thing. It is undeniable that the president requires a great deal of power if he is to deal successfully with the myriad concerns of the federal government, attempt to control the federal bureaucracy, persuade a status quo-oriented Congress of the need for his legislative program, etc. What the more-power-to-the-president-the-better school of thought has ignored is the corollary that the president needs additional power *where he does not already have sufficient power to function as the primary leader within a democratic system of government.* A democratic system means not only that the people possess the sovereign power, but that there is always someone around to watch those to whom the people have delegated their power and to make sure that those so delegated do not abuse their trust. Congress may be maddening in its occasional bursts of reactionary fervor, it may be far too responsive to the self-serving demands of interest groups, it may sometimes appear to delight in obstructing the president and the path of progress—but it is the only institution that can possibly keep presidential power within bounds on a day-to-day basis. It is not necessary for Congress to increase its power, but the time has come for Congress to exercise some of the powers which it has always formally possessed but which have been permitted to all but wither away.

3

Unbalanced Power

The previous chapter suggested that the balance of power between president and Congress that was envisioned by the framers of the Constitution is no longer a reality. Presidential power has become dominant in foreign affairs, but it is the Congress which has gained the upper hand in domestic policy. As this chapter seeks to indicate, neither is desirable.

Presidential Power and Foreign Policy

One of the many picket-sign slogans carried by marchers supporting the United States' Vietnam policy has been "My country—love it or leave it." The notion that a citizen who finds himself in serious disagreement with some of the policies adopted by his government has no alternatives other than maintaining his silence or emigrating is so antithetical to the democratic philosophy as to require no rebuttal. It is interesting to speculate however what the reaction of the signcarriers would be if their protests were met by integrationists chanting "My country—love it or leave it." Obviously, the demand for unanimity and total obeisance to government on the part of the public is highly selective.

The adoption by "hawks" of this simplistic watchword (and this is not to suggest that some of the slogans adopted by doves are not equally simplistic) underlines a strange but pervasive American belief that partisanship is out of place in foreign affairs. Most Americans seem to have assumed, at least from the time of World War II, that it is absolutely vital to the security of the United States to present a unified front to the rest of the world. Like the siblings who fight furiously amongst themselves, but suddenly unite against an attacker from outside the family. Americans feel that publication of internal disputes over foreign policy can only make America's role abroad more difficult and is therefore improper and immoral.

This viewpoint is reflected in Congress, where there is a tendency to view such foreign policy matters as alliances, treaties, overseas bases, reactions to foreign crises, and military intervention (but not foreign aid, tariffs, domestic bases, or food surplus disposal abroad) as requiring bipartisan agreement. The idea stems partly from congressional deference to greater presidential access to information, partly from a desire not to embarrass the executive branch, which must negotiate with foreign nations, by indicating to the other participants that the United States is not firmly behind the president; and partly from the belief that a nation united in its foreign policy will appear to be stronger and more worthy of respect. It is also recognized that once the president has acted, partisan debate may threaten the success of actions he has taken and reduce American credibility abroad. Neither party wants to run the risk of having the president tell the nation that his foreign policy would have been successful or that the United States would have been more secure had it not been for the political machinations of that party.

This means that unless the president does something particularly outrageous, he is likely to face less opposition on foreign policy matters than he does where domestic issues are concerned. Congress may oppose the president where it sees no relationship between the prestige of the United States as a nation and the foreign policy matter at hand; for example, the amount of foreign aid to be expended in a particular year or the kind of tariffs to be levied. When matters of grave political and military consequences are involved, however, Congress is inclined to defer to the president.

One of the few major legislative actions that President Kennedy was able to wrest from Congress was the Senate's ratification of the nuclear test ban treaty. This success is in marked contrast to his record in such domestic areas as civil rights. It is true that there was a good deal of public interest in the test ban issue, with mothers frightened about the amount of strontium-90 their children might be ingesting with their milk. It is also true that the attention of the American public was focused on the dramatic events of the civil rights movement, but that Congress did little about the president's proposed civil rights bill until after his death. It is arguable that the bill might not have passed without the emotion engendered by the assassination. It is true that the treaty required only Senate action, traditionally an easier road for presidential legislation than those House paths; but, the Senate with its filibusters proved to be the major hurdle for the civil rights bill. The only person who would have suffered embarrassment had the civil rights bill been voted down was the president who proposed it; had the test ban treaty been ratified by the so-called war-mongering Russians and voted down by the supposedly peace-loving Americans, the entire country would have been embarrassed. Even a president unable to extract much from a recalcitrant

Congress could manage to get the test ban treaty ratified. The clue to success lies in the different attitudes taken by both Congress and the public towards foreign and domestic affairs.

The axiom that the president must be supported no matter what and that we must stand united can be a dangerous one for the nation to cherish. One can speculate that much of the middle-level bureaucratic unhappiness with the Vietnam war might have received far more publicity—and might have had an important impact on the course of events—had governmental officials not felt compelled to silence their doubts about a national security matter. The difference between this situation and bureaucratic action in domestic affairs is easily seen if one considers the issue of the Nixon administration's integration policy. Governmental officials like Leon Panetta (director of the Civil Rights Office of the Department of Health, Education, and Welfare) and Paul Rilling (head of the Department's Southeastern bureau) resigned amid all the publicity they could generate. HEW civil rights workers demanded publicly that Secretary Finch meet with them to explain and defend the Department's policies. Gary Greenberg, an attorney in the Department's Civil Rights Division, refused in open court to defend the administration's integration policy. Members of the Department of HEW began meeting to see what they could do to alter the policy. Newspapers and news magazines speculated on the probable outcome of the discontent. Reporters were summoned to news conferences by resigning officials and, it seems clear, they were given a constant stream of "inside information" by those officials who remained.[1] When this is contrasted with the Indochina situation, the restraint exercised by dissenting bureaucrats becomes all the more remarkable. It is probably not, however, all the more desirable, assuming that day-to-day popular discussion of vital issues is part of the democratic process. The lack of real partisan opposition in foreign affairs may have led to a dangerous concentration of power in the presidency. The "checks and balances" existing for domestic issues are largely absent here.

An additional check on the president's power over domestic affairs, besides the ones exercised by the Congress, is public opinion. The average voter, whether or not he is truly informed, feels himself capable of evaluating governmental policy when ig directly concerns his home, hearth, and pocketbook. Many American newspapers carry a minimum of international news, but they all cover at least the major domestic stories. This, combined with their familiarity with earlier programs and their first-hand experiences, gives most voters a modicum of information about many domestic issues. They are not in the least hesitant about asserting that a proposed domestic program is all bad or that the president proposing it doesn't know what he's talking about. Popular sentiment about domestic issues is reflected in public opinion polls, letters to newspapers, and, to some extent, in congressional and presidential mail. When foreign policy matters are at issue, however, the average voter seems content to assume that his lack of expertise is inevitable because of the president's possession of greater knowledge, and particularly, secret knowledge. Thus another check on presidential power is absent.

American citizens do not possess much knowledge or understanding of foreign affairs partly because they are not much interested in acquiring it. They do not see themselves as directly affected by most foreign policies. Tariffs, for example, affect the price of the merchandise they buy, but one would be hard put to find ten average citizens who have any notion of what the United States' tariff policy is or what American tariffs already exist. Strikes which may make goods unavailable altogether, or increased Social Security benefits which affect the consumer's purchasing ability are another matter entirely. They are domestic issues and citizens are interested in their outcome.

The lack of American interest in foreign affairs can be simply proven by picking up newspapers representative of those published in the majority of American communities. Local news receives a great deal of coverage; much space is devoted to sports, comics, recipes, and the day's television schedule; important national stories may be reported in some detail, but the only international news coverage available is almost always extremely scanty and devoid of the kind of background information that makes international events comprehensible. European newspapers, by contrast, are full of international news. Americans are frequently amazed by the extent of the Europeans' knowledge of American issues and personalities. Whether American disinterest in foreign matters dates back to when the United States was largely an isolationist country, or whether it reflects a belief that since America is the biggest and the best, news of the outside world can't be terribly important, or whether it is the result of some other factor entirely, the fact remains that it enhances the president's ability to function far more independently than he can in the domestic sphere.

Yet another reason for increased presidential power is the relative absence of interest groups concerned about foreign affairs. Interest groups will appear in Washington if the government is considering tariff legislation or provisions in foreign aid bills that require receiving countries to use much of the aid to purchase American-made products, but where the vital issues of political alliances or military involvement are concerned, the number of groups clamoring to be heard is comparatively low. This frequently means that there is no countervailing power to offset the influence of the military-industrial establishment. To understand the extent to which American economic realities influence presidential decisions in this area, it is vital to consider the role played by the forces commonly called the military-industrial complex. Any examination of that complex must begin with money.

In 1957-1966, the profits after-tax of the American aerospace industry as a whole were 12.5 percent higher than those for American industry as an entity.[2] At the same time, production standards for the defense industries were extremely low. It is frequently unnecessary for them to deliver usable products or any products at all in order to make money, which is routinely advanced to them before work on a governmental contract is begun. Senator William O. Proxmire has discovered that out of 11 major weapons systems begun during the 1960s, only two electronic components performed up to expected standards, one at the 75 percent level, two at 50 percent, six at 25 percent or less.[3] These systems typically cost 200 to 300 percent more than the Pentagon estimated.[4] One firm, with failures on five of seven systems, earned 40 percent more than the rest of the aerospace industry and 50 percent more than industry as a whole.[5] In May 1969, a senior procurement officer for the Navy told a congressional subcommittee that there was serious waste and inefficiency in defense spending because of the military-industrial complex. According to his investigation, for example, the government could have saved $100 million on a contract for 3,000 aircraft engines if it had forced usual standards of industrial efficiency on the contractor. The price for the engines, which were later discarded, rose from an initial estimate of $273,910 each to a final figure of $750,000 each.[6] Even more startling, one corporation recently made a profit of 1,403 percent on an Air Force contract; its profits on 22 such contracts averaged 245 percent, ranging between 12.9 percent and the 1,403 percent mentioned.[7]

Defense contracts are the greatest boondoggle the government has to offer. They guarantee high profits even if the merchandise is unsatisfactory.[8] It might well be asked why, if defense contractors frequently prove inept at anything but making money, the government does not insist on higher standards. Part of the answer is to be found in certain employment statistics. As of February 1969, 2,124 former officers of the rank of Navy captain, Army colonel, or higher, were working for defense contractors; 210 were employed by Lockheed, 141 by McDonnell Douglas, 113 by General Dynamics, 169 by Boeing, and 104 by North American Rockwell. These are all major defense firms.[9] The former officers' contacts within the current military establishment are invaluable to the defense contractors. Current officers are not inclined to be too hard on their old buddies if the firms don't live up to their commitments, but they are inclined to throw business their way. Executives from the defense companies often move from the private sector into the public sector, just as old generals just fade away into private employment. David Packard, the deputy secretary of defense, for example, is the former chairman of the Hewlett-Packard Company, a major defense contractor.

The cozy relationship between former-military-men-turned-executives and former-executives-turned-bureaucrats is further sweetened by the avid desire of many congressmen for defense projects for their districts. Defense contracts mean new jobs, which mean new wages that will be spent in local stores, which means the creation of additional jobs in the local stores, etc., and the congressman who can claim that his influence in Washington was responsible for the whole thing is a congressman who has a good chance of reelection. Defense contracts imply the expenditure of vast amounts of public money, and this in turn implies that Congress must be willing to appropriate such sums. It is an open secret in Washington that the military, dependent for its importance upon continued congressional acquiescence in an ever-growing defense establishment, makes sure that the chairmen and influential members of key committees are properly looked after. Servicemen may be detailed for their personal use as valets and chauffeurs; military aircraft are made available to them and their families. And so, with mutual benefit to the armed forces, the defense industries and the Congress, the military-industrial establishment rolls on. Even Dwight Eisenhower, who spoke forcefully about very little during his presidency and who had enjoyed an outstandingly successful career in the military, utilized the occasion of his last presidential address to the public to warn about the frightening growth of the military-industrial complex.*

There are few pressure groups in Washington to balance the influence of the military-industrial establishment. That establishment is constantly pressing for new and bigger weapons, and money; there are no organized voices speaking for deescalation, for the lowering of our military profile, for the rerouting of military funds to domestic purposes. The lack of such voices means two things: first, there are no adequate checks and balances in this realm, and the power of the military-industrial complex is virtually unchallenged; and second, there is a built-in propensity for Washington to adopt a militaristic stance. This is a threat to the presidency, no matter what the particular policies of any president may be.

If a president wishes to minimize sword-rattling and the military arsenal he will find that it is an extremely difficult if not completely impossible task. Congress has been known to appropriate money for weapons that the president considers unnecessary but that the armed services want, and to "direct" the president to spend the money as appropriated. Congress may or may not have the constitutional authority to direct the president to act in such a manner and presidents have so far managed to handle the problem without provoking a confrontation between the two branches, but the point remains that Congress can usually be counted on as a staunch ally for the military whenever the president attempts to downgrade it.

If on the contrary, the president chooses to involve himself and the country in a militaristic endeavor, there will be too few Washington voices raised in dissent. When a president proposes a domestic program, those individuals and groups within the population who feel threatened by it will flock to Washington. They will seek out presidential assistants whenever that is possible; they will certainly lobby in the halls of Congress. The White House is involved in changes made in proposed bills while those bills are working their way through the legislative process. If interest groups have raised enough valid points or have mustered enough support to persuade congressmen to alter bills, the White House will know about it. The president can use the hearings of congressional

---

*While the obvious reasons the military-industrial establishment eschews publicity for its activities, occasionally it surfaces. The occasions are always highly instructive. One occurred on August 12, 1970, when 1,150 leaders of the establishment—congressmen, top military men, defense contractors, and Vice-President Agnew—gathered at a Washington hotel to honor Congressman L. Mendel Rivers. Mr. Rivers, whose South Carolina district is saturated with defense installations, was chairman of the House Armed Services Committee and a great friend of the defense establishment. The group was assembled to see Rivers receive the "Distinguished American Award" of the Washington Chapter of the Air Force Association. Entertainment was provided by Air Force bands and the Army's Old Guard Fife and Drum Corps.[10]

committees as a sampling of public opinion and decide what compromises he will have to make in the bill if it is to be enacted. In addition, defense contractors are important contributors to congressional campaign chests. Thus the legislative machinery, including the opportunity for interest groups to be heard, constitutes part of the bargaining process and prevents presidential power from becoming absolute.

There are only a few groups, however, which lobby for peace or for nonintervention in foreign affairs. The only quarrels that congressmen are apt to hear when military appropriations bills appear before them are those among the branches of the armed forces, with each branch contending that it does not have an adequate share of the pie. Compromise in such a situation is likely to consist of spreading the wealth around in a more satisfactory manner rather than in cutting back on the amount of wealth distributed. A president whose policies maximize the importance of the armed forces will inevitably discover that he has a friend in the military-industrial establishment. He will also find himself deprived of the kind of interest group activity that can add immeasurably to his ability to see the flaws in his own proposed bills and to understand how the country as a whole is likely to react to the legislation as enacted.

Congressional Power and Domestic Policy

Congressman Howard W. Smith first entered the House of Representatives in 1939. In 1958, he became chairman of the House Rules Committee. A "rule" in congressional parlance refers to a place on the agenda. No pending legislation can be discussed on the floor of the House until it is awarded a rule by the committee, which also establishes the procedure for floor debate and voting (e.g. whether or not amendments can be offered from the floor) and the time to be allotted for discussion. Until 1967, the committee chairman had the power to set meeting dates — which implies the power to postpone dates if the chairman does not want a bill to be discussed at all — and to table pending bills — another technique for burying proposed legislation. Congressman Smith utilized his power first as a committee member and then as chairman to bottleneck President Roosevelt's Wages and Hours Bill, emasculate as much of President Truman's Fair Deal as was possible, kill President Eisenhower's and President Kennedy's education and welfare measures, and personally delay Alaskan statehood for almost a year. He wielded much of his power even after 1961 when President Kennedy and Speaker Sam Rayburn barely managed to get the House to agree to enlarge the Rules Committee by two liberal members. Congressman Smith represented a district estimated in the 1966 *Congressional Directory* as having a 1960 population of 357,461.

In 1962, the House and the Senate passed somewhat different versions of the bills appropriating funds for governmental agencies. As is usual in such a case, a conference committee meeting was called. The only question to be resolved before the committee could do its work was where it would meet. Congressman Clarence Cannon of Missouri, chairman of the House Appropriations Committee and a venerable 83 years of age, thought it should meet in his office. Senator Carl Hayden, who had been a member of Congress since Arizona joined the Union and who was chairman of the Senate Appropriations Committee and an equally venerable 84, insisted that the meeting take place in *his* office. Cannon would not deign to enter the Senate nor Hayden the House. The feud raged for four months, during which some government agencies were left without the funds to meet their payrolls.[11]

These are but two examples out of many, and not the most outrageous examples, of the fantastic power exercised by congressional committee chairmen. While the power of the Rules Committee chairman was curbed to some extent when William Colmer acceded to the chairmanship; he still possesses considerable power. In 1970, Congressman Colmer, who represents a district in Mississippi, decided that he would not allow the House to vote on a bill giving the government power to enforce nondiscrimination in employment. Colmer simply declined to schedule a hearing on the bill which then languished and died. The power of the other chairmen remains unaltered. No tax reform bill has a chance of passage unless it has the support of Wilbur Mills, chairman of the House Ways and Means Committee. After President Nixon proposed his revenue-sharing plan to the nation, Congressman Mills serenely announced that he would schedule a committee hearing for it, but only for the purpose of killing it. What he meant, simply, was that the House would never vote on the bill because he would bury or alter it beyond recognition in his committee. President Nixon's welfare reform proposals could not have gotten through the House (or even onto the floor of the House) without Mills' consent. Chairman W. R. Poage of the House Agricultural Committee does not believe in giving away food to poor people, which is the major reason that the food stamp program is still so limited. Chairman John J. Rooney of the Subcommittee on State, Justice, Commerce, and the Judiciary of the House Appropriations Committee does not believe that overseas representatives of the American government should be given adequate expense and entertainment budgets, which is one reason why only wealthy men can afford to serve as American ambassadors.

Too many discussions of presidential versus congressional power overlook the fact that congressional power is the power of congressional committees and their chairmen rather than the power of the Congress as a whole. Visitors to Washington are invariably disappointed when they peer down over the railing of the gallery in the Senate or the House and discover that there are almost no elected officials on the floor. Many of the absent legislators are busy doing the real work of the Congress, which takes place in committee rooms. The *Congressional Record* is a thick document only because legislators are not required to actually present on the floor the speeches, articles, etc., which they insert in it. Each house occasionally musters a majority of its members for a vote; most of the time, however, the legislators are at work deciding the fate of proposed laws in committee.

Each house has its own procedure for the selection of committee members, but both adhere in great part to the seniority principle. In 1953, Lyndon Johnson, then Senate Majority Leader, propounded what became "the Johnson Rule." This established the policy of giving each freshman senator a place on at least one major committee. Although the rule continues to be followed, key positions on all committees remain in the hands of senior members, and chairmanships are assigned only to those with the greatest seniority. We have already seen that it is the representatives of one-party districts and states who are most likely to attain seniority and that it is precisely the one-party areas which are most likely to be at odds with an urban-oriented president. This factor, added to the great power given committee chairmen, results in conflict between the president and the powerful figures who control a few key committees. The major battle faced by a president is often getting a bill out of committee, rather than getting it enacted once it reaches the floor. Thus power struggles between the president and congressional committees are far more frequent than are power struggles between president and the Congress as a body.

One of the privileges of seniority is being able to choose one's committee assignments. A legislator is not likely to ask for a position on the Agriculture Committee if he represents an overwhelmingly urban constituency, nor is he wont to request assignment to the Banking and Currency Committee unless banking institutions play an important role in his district. Obviously, those legislators whose constituents have a stake in one aspect of the status quo will gravitate toward those committees where they can best serve their constituents. Those legislators whose constituents have a strong political commitment — against additional taxes for any purpose, against civil rights, or for minimized governmental involvement in economic affairs — will naturally seek positions on the committees which control legislation in areas relevant to their commitments. It is no accident that so many senior Southerners serve on the Senate Judiciary Committee, which controls civil rights legislation, or that so many rural district Southerners serve on the House Agricultural Committee. When the president proposes legislation designed to benefit *his* constituency, i.e., the urban (and suburban) majority, he is bound to run up against the entrenched bastions of special interests that constitute many congressional committees.

The interests entrenched in the committees are primarily domestic interests, as was noted before. The president will therefore discover that it is not only the American people who prefer to concentrate on domestic affairs; it is their representatives as well. It is in the domestic area that he wil have the most difficult going. Both Presidents Truman and Kennedy discovered this. President Johnson was able to wrest a large package of domestic legislation from the Congress that he swept in with him in 1964, but even his domestic successes were finally halted when the country became embroiled in Vietnam.

From the viewpoint of institutional power, there is nothing wrong with Congress deciding that the president's ideas are incorrect and that his legislation should be defeated. While there is nothing morally right or wrong about exercising power, danger lies in the tendency to misuse great accumulations of power. There is danger in the president's ability to involve the country in undeclared wars; there is equal danger in the ability of congressional committees to prevent the entire Congress from voting on presidential proposals. The president, with his large staff, flow of information, popular prestige, and potential for maximum exposure, is more than a match for the sprawling, decentralized mass of political bodies that is Congress. But unfortunately, he is no match for tightly organized congressional committees or committee chairmen who have near-absolute authority to block bills.

This seems to be the situation which, although not articulated, causes so many president-watchers to lament the power of Congress. If every committee was required to report out all bills submitted to it, with full provision made for the publication and circulation of minority reports, much of this dissatisfaction would disappear. Rural districts are still overrepresented in the House; the coalition of Southern Democrats and Northern Republicans does remain a threat to presidential legislation, particularly if it deals with social justice; but a president who was guaranteed a floor vote on all of his proposals would undoubtedly see more of his domestic legislation successfully enacted. A reduction in the power of congressional committees without a reduction in the power of Congress to vote down presidential requests would mean a far better balance between president and Congress in the area of domestic affairs.

Summary

A combination of congressional deference and public apathy has resulted in dangerously increased presidential power in most aspects of foreign affairs. Conversely, the ability of congressional committees to bottleneck legislation has resulted in a dangerous concentration of congressional power in many aspects of domestic affairs. The first is dangerous because the president can conclude alliances and commit forces unilaterally, without resorting to the bargaining process which is vital to the responsible use of power; the second is dangerous because small groups of congressmen can prevent the country from taking the steps necessary to translate social change into political change. If, as seems possible, the Congress acts to reassert its authority in the foreign arena, the first imbalance may be corrected.[12] It is questionable, however, whether the restored balance will last beyond the war in Indochina. It is assumed here that it is a matter of "when" rather than "if" the United States extricates itself from large-scale military involvement in Southeast Asia. Assuming that it does not become involved in another similarly unwinnable and unpopular guerila war somewhere else, public interest in the president's foreign affairs power will probably return to its usual low level and congressional attention will consequently wane. This will in turn leave the way clear for another eventual Vietnamlike presidential commitment, or perhaps, some misuse of the presidential power over foreign affairs not now envisioned. Given at least a temporary pause in America's overseas forays, the congressional committees' control over domestic affairs may come to seem far more significant.

4

Bureaucratic Power: A Complicating Factor

If Congress has climbed to awesome pinnacles of power in the struggle to control domestic affairs, another institution barely mentioned in the Constitution has amassed so much power that it has become one of the president's major competitors. That institution is the sprawling mass of men, programs, and money that constitutes the federal bureaucracy. As will become apparent, the major check on presidential power may well be an alliance among the Congress, the bureaucracy, and the special interest groups.

One of the great problems faced by any president today is the job, at once necessary and impossible, of controlling the bureaucracy. It is doubtful that any one human being could truly direct the day-to-day functioning of two and a half million people, even if the workers' allegiance and loyalty were to him alone. In reality, the bureaucracy is a great jousting-place for challenges from the warriors of many competing camps. In this arena, the president is merely one competitor among many, and history shows that he is far from the strongest.

Foremost among those with an interest in the operation of the executive agencies is their natural objects; namely those whose conduct the agencies must oversee. Farmers and farm groups, for example, are particularly concerned with the workings of the Department of Agriculture and its enforcement of particular farm programs and with the Army Corps of Engineers and the Bureau of Reclamation, both of which have authority over irrigation projects, etc. Policy is only potential until it is actually applied, at which time the kind of enforcement it receives can dramatically alter the official policy; therefore, interest groups keep close watch on the agencies charged with enforcing programs which are of

41

importance to them. At the same time, they recognize that the official policy can limit the parameters of possible action; therefore, they are concerned with the bills originating in congressional subcommittees. Congressmen, in turn, ask for assignments to specific committees and subcommittees because the activities of the committees are of particular concern to important elements of their constituency. Congressmen will be judged in large measure on the basis of what they have done for their constituents: a congressman from cotton-growing country is expected to fight for the highest possible subsidies for cotton growers and against duty-free importation of foreign cotton products. Knowing that if he loses a fight in Congress he may still be able to win it, or at least mitigate the harm done by his loss, as a new program works its way through the bureaucracy, a congressman thus is naturally eager to maintain close ties with the bureaucratic agencies relevant to his interests. The desire is mutual. The agencies depend upon their friends in Congress to fight for budgets, increased personnel, fields of jurisdiction, etc. It is the interest groups for which he fights in Congress and within the bureaucracy that can be expected to contribute to a congressman's campaign chest, so there is yet another political factor to the relationship. Nevertheless, politics aside, the common interest, be it cotton farming, military armaments, urban redevelopment, or whatever, shared by the congressman, the bureaucrat, and the pressure group makes it logical for them to work together. It is from this three-way relationship that much of the federal policy toward their common interest will develop. As a unit, the three-sided group will have a great deal of collective expertise on the matter. It will also, of course, have a particular bias: for existing programs, for new programs that will benefit the interest group, and against threats to curtail the power of jurisdiction of the relevant bureaucratic agency, etc. When one realizes that these three-way groups exist vis-à-vis most aspects of American life, one can understand the difficulty a president invariably faces in overseeing his mammoth and multi-motivated bureaucracy.

The officials designated by the president to run the bureaucracy for him, cabinet members, subcabinet officials, etc., share many of the disadvantages faced by the president. Their jobs are dependent upon him, which means that their tenure will be at most as short as his. The great majority of federal bureaucrats are members of the civil service system which means in effect that they have their jobs for the duration of their working lives. Each president and his appointees will be factors in the bureaucrats' jobs for no more than eight years under normal circumstances. If the bureaucrats don't approve of presidential policies, their natural inclination is to stall as long as possible in the hope that the president's tenure will be over before he gets around to making a concerted effort to change their way of doing things. More importantly, the real power in each bureaucracy lies with the middle-level management: those civil servants who make the day-to-day decisions and keep the bureaucracy functioning in spite of the vagaries of electoral politics. It is usually with these middle-level managers that the relevant congressional committees meet for their annual review sessions. Occasionally, such figures as assistant secretaries will join in the sessions; more frequently, the bureaucracy is represented by senior career employees. The same senior career people who deal daily with the same interest groups will meet yearly with the same congressional committee. Agreements over which programs will be stressed and how others will be implemented are frequently made at the meetings (and, of course, contacts between the legislators and the bureaucrats are hardly confined to once-a-year meetings).

It is thus usually the career bureaucrats rather than the president or his representatives who form the frame of reference within which the committee works. Even when a subcabinet official manages to exercise a certain amount of control, he, because of presidential acceptance of nominees tendered by particular congressmen or presidential desire to seek out men with expertise or both, may well be inclined toward the views of the unofficial triumverate rather than the views of the president. Clarence D. Palmby, for example, was an associate administrator of President Eisenhower's Commodity Stabilization Service which administered the commodity subsidy programs. He then worked as the executive vice-president of the United States Feed Grains Council, a lobbying group for the farmers who are the beneficiaries of federal subsidy and surplus commodity programs. When President Nixon took office, Palmby became the assistant secretary of International Affairs and Commodity Programs in the Agriculture Department—charged with enforcing the government's policies toward the very people for whom he had just been lobbying. Clearly, the relationship among Palmby, the congressional agriculture committees, the farm groups, and the Agriculture bureaucracy predated the policies of the Nixon administration and could be expected to continue after the end of the administration. This is but one example among many.

It is the greatest achievement of the American bureaucratic system that it continues to function no matter what happens on the electoral scene. In the interim between the election of a new president and his inauguration policy decisions are suspended and leadership from the top is minimal, but bureaucracy goes on grinding out its papers, orders, checks, and directives. Its self-contained nature, however, makes it impossible for a president to assume that seasoned bureaucrats will simply carry out his orders without extensive prodding and persuasion. Additionally, tradition and bureaucratic in-fighting may subvert any presidential purpose. President Kennedy was faced with a dramatic example of this during the Cuban missile crisis. As early as 1961, he had talked about his desire to remove obsolete American missiles from Turkey. Various political considerations led to delays in the issuing of an order until August 1962, at which time he directed that the missiles be removed immediately. The State and Defense Departments disagreed and were not particularly anxious to carry out the order. In addition, the bureaucracies of both departments had developed a comfortably slow-moving tradition. To Kennedy's great dismay, he discovered in the midst of the missile crisis in October 1962 that the missiles in Turkey had not yet been removed and were a bargaining point for the Russians.[1]

Earlier, he had come up against the State Department's slow-moving procedures when he asked State to draft a reply from him to a note from Premier Khruschev. He was thoroughly annoyed to find that it took the department 43 days to draft a note which contained none of the language that Kennedy himself had suggested be used.[2] He also discovered that he could not necessarily trust State Department evaluations of problem situations, since secrecy often prevented department officials dealing with a problem from knowing about other problems that might have an important bearing on it.[3] State's techniques not only caused annoyance at home; they also created confusion abroad. Kennedy found some instructions issued by a supercautious State Department to Ambassador John K. Galbraith to be such a useless collection of cliches that he threw them into his wastebasket.[4] State's struggles for power with other bureaucracies created additional problems. During the Kennedy administration, each American agency represented in Laos had its own program and personnel. Their ideas about the best American policy in Laos frequently differed and ideological battles were fought both in Laos and Washington. Eventually, the CIA and the Defense Department formed an alliance, with AID and the State Department on the other side. All four firmly maintained the bureaucratic tradition of carrying out their duties with far more regard for their own points of view than for basic American policy. Ambassadors who were assigned to Laos tended to choose either the CIA-Defense side or the AID-State side, and no one in Laos could really tell which faction actually spoke for the United States.[5] The president may have thought the United States had a coherent Laotian policy, but the bureaucrats disagreed, and since it was the bureaucrats who were entrusted with carrying out the policies, it was they who were correct.

Kennedy ran into particular difficulties with the foreign-policy bureaucracy partly because it had operated almost autonomously during the Eisenhower years and partly because he was especially concerned with altering the underlying assumptions of American foreign policy. Each agency provides its own obstacles, but every element in the bureaucracy presents the same problem of control to the president.

Congressmen and interest groups tend to be even more influential with the bureaucracies that oversee domestic rather than foreign affairs. The federal free school-lunch program, created by statute, includes guidelines on the family income and size of the family of the children participating in the program. No questions unrelated to these guidelines are supposed to be asked of the child or his family. Nevertheless, the application form provided by one Georgia school includes the questions, "Would you be willing to let your children do a small amount of work, such as picking up paper, as part payment for the lunches they receive? Are you willing to allow a committee from the PTA to visit your home to investigate this application for free lunches?" Both questions are illegal, but were approved by the United States Department of Agriculture bureaucrats administering the program.[6] The Senate Select Committee on Nutrition found that many of the nutrition programs were not reaching the people for whom they were intended, primarily because of negligent and/or negative administrative practices,[7] and that in many instances they were being administered illegally. For example, children receiving federally-supported free lunches in some New York schools are forced to eat separately from other children or to use different lines or different-colored lunch tickets—all contributing to an illegal singling-out of the program's beneficiaries.[8] A 1969 study found that the money appropriated for lunches for 1,000,000 children was feeding only 400,000, with more than half the money being diverted elsewhere.[9] The USDA bureaucracy must work closely with Congressman W. R. Poage of Texas, the chairman of the House Agriculture Committee, who does not believe in giving food to hungry children. When another congressman protested against Poage's opposition to the food stamp program, arguing that "I don't want to feed bums, but neither do I think we should visit the sins of the parents upon the children," Congressman Poage replied, "You didn't make that law, Mr. Foley. That law came from a higher authority. That law has lasted throughout history. You aren't going to change that law."[10] It was also Chairman Poage who commented, during one hearing on the food stamp program, that too many supporters of the program were "concerned in maintaining a bunch of drones" and added,

> You know what happens in the beehive. They kill those drones. That is what happens in most primitive societies. Maybe we have just gotten too far away from the situation of primitive man.[11]

Poage ordered those remarks stricken from the official record of the hearing, but in spite of the political sensitivity that action indicates, it is not surprising that the food stamp programs of both the Johnson and Nixon administrations have been aborted largely by the Poage-influenced USDA bureaucracy.

However, other bureaucracies do not present equal challenges to presidential control. The extent of the challenge depends on the amount of time that the bureaucracy has had to entrench itself and on the political influence of its members. President Kennedy had great trouble with the State Department; President Nixon however had no difficulty at all with the Departments of Justice and Health, Education and Welfare in reversing integration policies by "purging" those Departments of large numbers of dissenters.

As always, there is more than one side to any story. Just as Congress occasionally passes legislation that it would be politically unwise to oppose, then hopes and expects that the Supreme Court will declare it unconstitutional, so too the president can take advantage of the slow-moving bureaucratic machinery to cripple his own programs. The Commission on Civil Rights discovered that in spite of the pro civil rights attitude of the top echelons of the Johnson administration and of the president himself, much of the civil rights legislation passed during their tenures was never effectively enforced. Part of the blame lies with slow-moving bureaucrats motivated by their personal antipathies and congressional pressures, but the president who did not make use of his executive power is also to blame. Political pressures and personal inclinations encouraged the president to give civil rights legislation top priority. It can be speculated, however, that opposing political pressures led to his failure to direct the bureaucracy once the legislation was enacted. The administration received credit for the legislation, but the intended beneficiaries of the legislation found that in many areas little real benefit was forthcoming.

On the whole, lack of bureaucratic response is far more of a problem than a blessing for the president. While there is no question that the bureaucracy should not be allowed to systematically sabotage the enforcement of enacted legislation, it ought to be pointed out that there may be residual benefits in relative bureaucratic independence. The employees in the civil rights divisions of the Departments of Justice and HEW who continued to try to enforce federal legislation after the Nixon administration took office, and until it purged many of them, did so in spite of the fact that any meaningful enforcement activity conflicted with administration policy. In this instance, the fragmented nature of the control of the bureaucracy was a boon to social justice. Usually, it is not, simply because the special interest groups which take advantage of the fragmented power are, almost by definition, unconcerned with the impact of their influence on the majority of Americans. Any group which has spent sufficient time and money required to gain influence with the bureaucracy and Congress is necessarily interested in circumventing the more orthodox democratic processes. The pro civil rights bureaucrats exercised what power they could in the name of a group of people otherwise largely unrepresented. The usual situation finds bureaucrats involved in a three-way relationship[12] with groups whose congressmen represent them quite efficiently.

Thus the major check on presidential power may well be, not the Congress in its legislative capacity, but the Congress in its executive capacity allied with the bureaucracy and special interest groups. It is hardly necessary to point out that only one member of this triumverate—Congress—can claim to have been elected by the public and even congressmen concerned with a particular area of government activity function as a special interest group almost free of restraint from the Congress as a whole. This constitutes more than a problem for presidential power, it is also a challenge to the democratic process.

5

The Isolation of the Presidency: Staff, Cabinet, and Congress

On March 25, 1968, a group of elder statesmen and former high-ranking military men met in Washington at the special request of President Johnson.[1] Worried about indications that the Vietnam problem might make his election campaign exceedingly difficult and concerned about Pentagon demands for the deployment of additional troops, the president asked the group to reassess the war effort. These men had given him the benefit of their counsel on many occasions since 1965 and were known as the "Senior Advisory Group on Vietnam." Among those present at the meetings and briefings on March 25 and 26 were such men as former Secretary of State Dean Acheson, former Under-Secretary of State George Ball, former Presidential Special Assistant McGeorge Bundy, former Deputy Secretary of Defense Cyrus Vance, former Joint Chiefs of Staff Omar Bradley and Maxwell Taylor, former Senator and Ambassador to Saigon Henry Cabot Lodge, Supreme Court Justice Abe Fortas, and United Nations Ambassador Arthur Goldberg. They read a number of background papers; dined at the State Department where they were briefed by such top officials as Secretary of State Rusk, Presidential National Security Assistant Walt W. Rostow, and Richard Helms, the director of the CIA; and then moved on to the Operations Center of the State Department where they heard from middle-echelon officials like Philip Habib of the State Department, George Carver of the CIA, and Joint Chiefs staff member Major General William Depuy. The latter group had no access to the president. After hearing what seems to have been a startlingly pessimistic report, the Senior Advisory Group met again the next morning to hear Secretary of Defense Clark Clifford argue against sending more troops to Vietnam, whereupon they went to the White House for lunch with the president. It was at the discussion following that the president discovered that most of the Group opposed the conduct of the war and felt that it had to be ended as quickly as possible through negotiations. Those who had previously applauded the war effort—Bundy, Acheson, Bradley, Vance, etc.—had completely reversed their earlier views; only three men dissented from the Group's reappraisal. The president is described as being "visibly shocked,"[2] "stunned,"[3] and "appalled"[4] —largely because he realized that the Group had come to its decision on the basis of information not directly available to him.

Lyndon Johnson got much of his information about the progress of the war from Walt W. Rostow, who not only played a key role in selecting the written information on foreign policy matters that Johnson read, but also helped decide which experts the president would see. Rostow is credited by Under-Secretary of the Air Force Townsend Hoopes with being so selective, influential, and passionate a supporter of the war effort that he and the information he channeled to President Johnson were instrumental in widening the credibility gap.[5] Theodore White contends that the only advice on Vietnam that the president heard came to him via Rostow, Rusk, McNamara (while he was secretary of defense), and top military leaders;[6] while George Christian reports that Johnson maintained an unwavering faith in Dean Rusk and that no matter who else he may have consulted, he depended upon Rusk's judgment.[7] Louis Heren, the respected Washington correspondent for the *London Times,* agrees that the president relied far too heavily on the Pentagon for information, sending few personal envoys to Vietnam to report on the situation independently, and accepting too readily data from the American ambassador in Saigon and the CIA, both parts of the war machine.[8] Thus the credibility gap can be seen as resulting from a bit of Texas political optimism and a great deal of presidential misinformation.

While the United States was engaged in a major military effort that enraged many of its allies and turned its citizens into two snarling camps, each convinced of the evil intentions of the other; while troops were drafted and over 30,000 of them died and hundreds of thousands were wounded; while millions of Vietnamese civilians were wounded, maimed, killed, and turned into homeless refugees; while young men became draft-dodgers and spent their time in federal prisons or fled to Canada or Sweden; while the costs of the war mounted and inflation spiralled; the president of the United States, the chief executive and commander-in-chief, made his decisions about the war on the basis of inadequate and faulty information. He had systematically isolated himself from anybody but supporters, most of them men whose positions were dependent upon his will.[9]

One of the things that appears to have intrigued Richard Nixon upon moving into the White House is staff organization. He has made a few changes, but his primary aim seems to have been the creation of a completely rational hierarchy with clear lines of responsibility and command. The names of some of the players have changed, but the basic pattern emerges. Central to the scheme again is the relative isolation of the president. As of this writing, four members of his White House staff have unlimited access to him: H. R. Haldeman, his chief of staff, who monitors the visitors to the Oval Office and the telephone calls that the president accepts; John D. Ehrlichman, former counsel and current director of the Domestic Council, who is Nixon's chief adviser on domestic affairs; Henry A. Kissinger, assistant to the president for national security affairs and his chief adviser on foreign policy; and George P. Shultz, promoted from secretary of labor to the newly created post of director of the Office of Management and Budget. Haldeman serves as a watchdog with almost total control over who Nixon sees and what he reads.[10] Former Secretary of the Interior Walter J. Hickel apparently holds Haldeman responsible for restricting Hickel's access to the President.[11] Kissinger reviews the communications which wind up on the president's desk from the Departments of Defense and State and the CIA. The National Security Council staff, greatly expanded from that commanded by President Johnson and now numbering over 30 assistants, always reports to Kissinger and rarely even sees the president. The counselors to the president see the president with varying frequency and funnel requests to see him through Haldeman or Ehrlichman. All domestic policy matters requiring major presidential decisions must be submitted via Ehrlichman. When the president holds his eight o'clock morning meetings to plan the day's activities, it is reportedly Haldeman, Shultz, Ehrlichman, Kissinger, Robert H. Finch, and Donald Rumsfeld (presidential assistant and director of the Office of Economic Opportunity) who are regularly present.[12]

President Nixon does not make a practice of reading a representative sample of the nation's newspapers, or watching television news commentators. Each day, a staff of six working under speech writer Patrick H. Buchanan gives the president a summary of the news articles, columns, and editorials that they think are important. The summary includes quotes and may run between 20 and 40 pages, but it is chosen by Buchanan et al., just as the president's other reading material is largely chosen by Haldeman, Ehrlichman, and Kissinger.[13]

President Nixon does not read his mail. Obviously, no president can deal with the thousands of letters that pour into the White House each week. Seventeen analysts sort them, and the President is given a report on the way his mail is running, along with a cross-section of about 40 letters each week.

During the first two years of his administration, President Nixon did not meet regularly with his cabinet or with its individual members. The unsuccessful attempt made by Secretary Hickel to speak with the president about the reaction of young Americans to the Cambodian invasion and the rebuff he received from the White House staff (and, of course, his eventual dismissal) is perhaps the most widely reported episode of its kind, but it is indicative of the president's attitude towards most of his cabinet members. After a good deal of press comment on the president's relation to his cabinet, and subsequent to the firing of Hickel and Hickel's charge that the president was isolating himself to the extent of "just sitting around and listening to his staff,"[14] President Nixon promised the cabinet that beginning in 1971 he would meet with it every two weeks.[15] Whether these meetings occur and whether they will be more than pro forma remains to be seen.

President Nixon reportedly wanders off to a secluded office with a yellow legal pad in hand whenever a major decision has to be made. "Secluded" in this context is a relative term, for it is clear that even outside of his special isolation chamber he leads a highly secluded existence. His most frequent visitors, and the men upon whom he is primarily dependent, are a small number of White House assistants.

The particular names and incidents that appear above and in what follows are drawn primarily from the first two years of the Nixon administration. The names and the formal organizational lines may well change, especially as President Nixon seems inclined to tinker with the machinery of the White House staff. Unfortunately, a change in the players will not materially alter the game. A president uninterested in obtaining advice from a broad ideological spectrum will remain isolated no matter who he is, or who his most favored advisers may be. This applies not only to the current president, but to those who follow him as well. Even President Kennedy, who was concerned with the quality and representativeness of the advice available to him, had to constantly fight against the built-in isolation of the presidency. This is made evident by a passage in Robert Kennedy's *Thirteen Days*.[16] In reflecting upon the Cuban missile crisis, Kennedy discusses the "cowering effect" that the presidential office seems to have on those who come near it and the way in which otherwise intelligent and forceful men alter their opinions to coincide with those of the president. Kennedy saw advisers do precisely this during the administrations of both his brother and President Johnson. As illustration, he relates the following:

> I once attended a preliminary meeting with a Cabinet officer, where we agreed on a recommendation to be made to the President. It came as a slight surprise to me when, a few minutes later, in the meeting with the President himself, the Cabinet officer vigorously and fervently expressed the opposite point of view, which, from the discussion, he quite accurately learned would be more sympathetically received by the President.[17]

One gathers that his surprise was only "slight" because the incident was not unique.

The White House Staff

The White House Office came into existence as an official entity in 1939, although presidents had employed a staff of aides and secretaries before that time. The White House staff exists within the Office and may be functionally defined as those White House employees not subject to Senate confirmation who are in personal contact with the president, or with those who are in contact with him, and who therefore play an active role in the presidential decision-making process. Each modern president has increased the size of the staff until, in the Nixon administration, it numbers about 50 presidential appointees and about 100 assistants to the appointees. The staff members have various titles: assistant to the president, presidential counsel, press secretary, Counselor to the president, etc. On paper, some of them derive their positions from small committees: the National Security Council, the Urban Affairs Council, the Environmental Quality Council, the Domestic Affairs Council. Some of the presidential advisers are specialists, but it is the generalists among them who are usually most influential (or, perhaps, the president's desire to use trusted men in a variety of capacities turns influential advisers into generalists). Most of the men who figure importantly in recent presidential history are, or have been members of the White House staff: O'Donnell, O'Brien, Sorensen, Schlesinger, Moyers, Jenkins, Valenti, Bundy, Rostow, Kissinger, Ehrlichman, Moynihan, Haldeman, Harlow, etc.

To understand both the usefulness of the White House staff and the dangers inherent in their positions, it is necessary to consider the professional world of the presidential adviser. If he is important enough to see the president frequently, his office is actually in the White House. His entire official raison d'être is his ability and willingness to serve the president. It is the president who appointed him to his position and it is the president who can dismiss him. The people whose opinions matter to the adviser consider him important because of his proximity to the power of the presidency. Outside the White House, he is listened to with respect, for it is always assumed that he is not speaking only for himself and that an alert ear can catch echoes of the president's thinking. Washington hostesses vie for his presence at dinner parties and Washington newsmen fastidiously scribble down his utterances. He shares the presidential jet, visits the presidential retreats, hears his importance speculated about on television. Should he lose his job, all this will suddenly be gone.

Given this second-hand power, the psychological pressure to tell the president what he wants to hear and to support those ideas which he favors must be enormous. The presidency is the supreme prize offered in American political life, but very few men can become president. For those to whom the White House is the symbol of the ultimate goal, the next best thing to the presidency itself is the role of presidential adviser. Those playing the role must suffer from the omnipresent, albeit subconscious knowledge that the fall from grace will be a very long and humiliating one. Under the circumstances, one can hardly expect the majority of advisers to escape the trap of yes-men. Even if they are sufficiently certain of their position to speak freely, the very factor that gives them that security may limit their usefulness. This can even happen to presidential aides who are unafraid of the president because they have known and worked with him long before he entered the White House.

As we will see, the peculiar role played by the cabinet permits the president to select men he barely knows for cabinet positions. He may not see particular cabinet members from one month to the next, so as long as they seem to be running their departments fairly well and eschewing loud disagreements with influential congressmen, he is content with their performance. The purpose of White House aides, however, is to work intimately with the president and to be ever available for whatever jobs he has. This places them at the very heart of the decision-making process and the presidency itself. Heren notes that after Kennedy's assassination, President Johnson begged Kennedy's staff to remain at their jobs, partly to insure continuity, but also because he realized that only they understood the president's job well enough to be of help to him.[18] McGeorge Bundy understood the complicated defense system so well that Johnson would have necessarily relied on him, rather than on the secretaries of state or defense had there been a military emergency[19] (and it must be remembered that in the post assassination days no one was certain whether or not the assassination represented the first stage in an all-out attack on the American government).

The president naturally wants those who are in close proximity to him and those on whose advice he must rely to be people he knows well, has learned to trust, and whose personalities mesh comfortably with his own. Johnson inherited both President Kennedy's White House staff and his cabinet. He was able to retain some cabinet members until the time he left Washington, but in spite of his early request that they stay, the White House staff had to be replaced one by one in a comparatively short period of time. Presidential aides with New England accents gave way to those who spoke with a Texas twang. Johnson could no more have worked happily with Kennedy's staff over any great length of time, than Kennedy could have worked with Johnson's. As Sorensen points out, the White House staff functions as additional hands, ears, and eyes for the president; of necessity, its members must be appointed for their "ability to fulfill the President's needs and talk the President's language."[20]

The implication is that the primary loyalty of the staff is to the president *as a person,* since in many cases the loyalty predates his presidency, rather than to the government or the executive branch as abstract institutions. Of course, presidential aides are inclined to assume that since the president almost always acts correctly, his actions are good for the government and the electorate, so that loyalty to him in no way precludes loyalty to the democratic ideal for them. Nevertheless, the tendency is to protect the president from the world beyond the White House gates, rather than to insist that he examine his policies to see whether they might be mistaken. Since the president, no matter who he is or what his policies may be, is the natural target for a great deal of anger and dissatisfaction, it is logical for his staff to attempt to protect him from destructive criticism. Unfortunately, "destructive" too easily becomes a catch-all for criticism that is really constructive. In addition, the ego of the staff members themselves may become involved, for the president's policies are the policies that they have helped to define, and criticism of him necessarily implies criticism of them.

Recent presidents have themselves recognized the problem, consciously or not, and have attempted in varying ways to institutionalize a steady flow of conflicting opinions. While no one has gone as far as Franklin Roosevelt in deliberately pitting adviser against adviser to profit from the quality of advice resulting from the competition, later presidents have sought advice outside the usual channels. President Johnson's penchant for picking up the telephone and asking friends outside the government for their opinions is well-known. It was only after he limited the circle of outside advisers to supporters of his Vietnam policy that the caliber of his decisions began to decline. President Kennedy scandalized some bureaucrats by his willingness to ignore the hierarchy of authority and seek out the opinions of those in the second or even third rank in the chain of command. He ordered copies of all important cables sent to and from the Departments of State and Defense and the CIA to be sent to the White House. He also sought information from ambassadors, reporters, officials who had recently traveled overseas, weekly department reports, newspapers, etc.[21] With the great exception of Vietnam for President Johnson, both Presidents Kennedy and Johnson tried to have important issues debated before them in order to be certain that they heard all the possible alternatives.

Their approaches to the decision-making process while differing in many details, reflected a desire to retain all possible power over policy decisions. The great contrast to this is the technique utilized by President Eisenhower who insisted that all arguments be reconciled and all points of view merged into a compromise position before a problem was set before him for final decision. The problem and its preferred solutions had to be compressed into as little reading matter as possible, and even than had to be approved by his second-in-command before being given to the president. Obviously, the amount of vital information that flowed into the Oval Office was extremely limited.

President Nixon came into office determined to steer a middle course. While he insisted on neat lines of authority and a clear table of organization, he announced his intention of reaching outside for the widest sampling of opinions. Unfortunately, his desire for organization seems to have triumphed over his thirst for information. Ehrlichman, Haldeman, and Kissinger are now expected to eliminate from the president's reading the information and the proposals that they feel are not of sufficient importance to claim any of his limited time. This inevitably means that to some extent their judgment is substituted for his. Unless the president is to read *everything,* which is obviously impossible, this kind of presifting is necessary. One criterion for evaluating this system, and the factor that helps to create great differences among presidents, is the extent to which the president insures that the White House hierarchy does not become his only source of information.

When President Nixon was faced with the decision of whether to deploy the antiballistic missile system, he relied primarily on Henry Kissinger, Defense Secretary Melvin Laird, Deputy Defense Secretary David Packard, Secretary of State William Rogers, Under-Secretary of State Elliot Richardson, and Director of the Arms Control and Disarmament Agency Gerard C. Smith for advice. Some of these men in turn relied upon others, with Kissinger's National Security Council playing a major role. The president saw personally almost no senators or scientists. Senators Jacob Javits, Charles Percy, and John Sherman Cooper managed to see Kissinger to register their opposition to deployment, but their words reached the president only through the summary of their views which Kissinger wrote for him. The president's assistant in charge of congressional liaison, Bryce Harlow, reportedly was not asked which of the alternatives under consideration would be most acceptable to the Senate.[22] This may appear to be a laudable example of policy-making from principle rather than political concerns, but to the extent that the Senate as a collective body is in closer touch with the electorate and less at the mercy of obsequious aides, it is also an example of policy-making without reference to the will of the people. Such debate as occurred was kept within the channels of government, with Kissinger assigning one of his aides to work up the arguments against deployment while the aide also helped Packard write out the options (and presumably the supporting arguments) for deployment.[23] The involvement of anyone outside the executive branch was kept at minimum. Once the decision was made, Nixon again isolated himself and relied on his congressional liaison staff to do whatever was necessary to get the bill through. He mistakenly depended on his staff (and the unreliable Democratic hierarchy in the House) for an evaluation of the kind of congressional support he would get. The result was that without the vice-president's vote, the Senate would have voted to turn down the president's deployment proposal and administration critics were given a rallying point for some years to come.

In their own ways, the White House staff members are as isolated as the president. The cocoon that separates him from the rest of the world is wrapped around his staff as well. They are caught up in the same issues, the same personalities, the same Washington milieu. Their information may be as faulty as his. Tom Wicker reports, for example, that one of President Johnson's White House assistants did not realize the extent of anti-Johnson sentiment among young people in general and students in particular until he left the White House.[24]

President Nixon in making his ABM decision did go beyond his staff to seek the aid of cabinet and subcabinet officials. The cabinet would seem to be a logical place for a president to look when he is searching for informants outside the White House. To what extent, then, can cabinet members minimize the president's isolation?

The Cabinet

Cabinet positions are offered for a variety of reasons. They may be given to those who the president simply wants near him, no matter what their official capacity, and who are capable of running an executive department. President Kennedy's appointment of his brother as attorney general is one example; President Nixon's appointment of John Mitchell to the same office is another. A secretaryship may be a reward for political services rendered, as in the case of Abraham Ribicoff, who had given Kennedy important support before the 1960 convention and who was named secretary of health, education and welfare, or Maurice Stans, who raised extraordinary amounts of money for Nixon's campaign fund and was rewarded with the office of secretary of commerce. It is almost traditional for the postmaster generalship to go to someone who has been extremely active in party affairs; indeed, the office was created precisely for this purpose.[25] In some instances, the men so rewarded may be of sufficient ability to merit the job on that ground alone; in other cases, this is far from true. Presidents may sometimes appoint men who are personally unknown to them on the basis of strong recommendations from advisers they trust. Both Secretary of State Dean Rusk and Secretary of Defense Robert McNamara, who were destined by history to play roles of immense importance in the Kennedy and Johnson administrations, were selected by President Kennedy in this manner. Party affiliation is clearly another major factor. Almost the entire cabinet will be members of the president's party, although recent custom favors including one opposition party member as a gesture of bipartisanship. Geography is also considered, with no section of the country being represented by a disproportionate share of cabinet positions, and with certain posts traditionally being reserved for certain regions of the country.

The history of the cabinet as an institution is illuminating, both in explaining an additional reason for cabinet appointments and in discussing the possible advisory role the cabinet can play. The only major executive positions created by the first Congress were the secretaryships of state, war, and treasury, and the office of attorney general. The first three were made heads of departments; the attorney general was given no department. Congress said nothing about these executives consituting a formal cabinet, although it was clear that they would each give the president the constitutionally mandated "opinion, in writing, of the principal officer in each of the executive departments" and therefore function as sources of information and advice. According to the leading authority on the cabinet[26] later departments were in large measure created as a result of social change which produced interest groups demanding presidential and congressional recognition of their problems. A primary method of extending such recognition was the establishment of an executive department complete with secretary who presumably had access to the presidential ear.

The secretary of agriculture represents the interests of the farmers; the secretary of commerce, the interests of business; and the secretary of labor, the interests of unions. The secretary of the treasury reflects the concerns of the financial world; the secretary of the interior, the concerns of those (primarily in the West) interested in preventing commercial exploitation of the land; the secretary of health, education, and welfare, the concerns of the social justice "establishment"; the secretary of housing and urban development, supposedly, the same "establishment" particularly the urban minorities; the secretary of transportation, those interested in bigger and better highways. The secretaries of state and defense are less parochial, but are frequently forced to expend a good deal of their time and energy attempting to control their respective bureaucracies. The Postmaster General hovers vaguely on the fringes of the group and the Attorney General, if he is not someone who could function as easily in the White House as in the Justice Department, concerns himself with the government's litigation and the drafting of proposed legislation. It is hardly surprising that the White House Office has grown enormously in size and importance as the president's major pool of advisers.

The president cannot expect objectivity from many members of his cabinet because they view all proposals from the vantage point of their particular constituencies. The secretaries of state and defense may be exceptions; but, as noted above, the deputy secretary of defense upon whom President Nixon relied so heavily during his ABM decision-making process is a former munitions maker. He cannot always expect expertise, especially when political considerations have played a stronger role in his appointments than the claims of talent. Attorney General John Mitchell ran Nixon's successful 1968 campaign, but he can scarcely claim expert knowledge of American popular opinion or of the most successful ways to mobilize congressional support. The president may discover that some of his cabinet members are highly intelligent and not overly abrasive, and he may come to rely upon them heavily as individuals. President Nixon is reported to discuss most of his decisions with Attorney General Mitchell, who is probably better informed about what the president is thinking than are many of his White House advisers, but he cannot use the cabinet as his primary source of advice.

What he can do, however, is recognize that the cabinet is an embodiment of American pluralism and utilize it accordingly. He can try out his ideas on his secretaries in order to see how the interests which they represent can be expected to react. He can use them as a source of feedback where the problems of major concern to various groups within the electorate find reflection. If his staff has begun to pay too little attention to the desires of one group or another, the appropriate cabinet member should be able to warn him of discontent before it becomes politically serious. Aside from the vital functions of running their own departments and seeing that the president's policies are carried out, this is the major reason for the existence of the cabinet. It enables the president to see past the walls of the Executive Mansion and beyond the boundaries of the Capitol District. It is an important source of information about the state of the country, especially since the existence of the White House staff minimizes the president's exposure to particular interest groups and factions. This is why a president who cuts himself off from his cabinet members adds dangerously to his own intellectual isolation.[27]

The Congress

One group that would certainly seem unafraid to let the president know when it disapproves of what he is doing and therefore would appear instrumental in linking the president with the world beyond the White House is Congress. Although a president who cuts himself off from Congress may not be successful in enacting his legislative program, that does not mean that he cannot isolate himself from Congress if he so wishes.

Every recent president has had an assistant whose primary job has been to handle congressional relations. In effect, the legislative liaison acts as the president's lobbyist on Capitol Hill. The size of Congress and the number of matters that concern president and Congress make it obvious that one liaison, or even two or three, cannot possibly handle the job alone. He can, however, pinpoint the areas of maximum disagreement or those instances where a particular congressman may be most amenable to argument and/or pressure and then pass on the job of actually making contact to another presidential aide, a cabinet or subcabinet member, a friendly congressman, etc. The president himself may be called upon to exert whatever pressure is implicit in his office, including threats or promises. President Johnson was well-known for his habit of telephoning recalcitrant congressmen when he was particularly interested in a piece of pending legislation. Presidential contacts with congressmen are institutionalized in the meetings the president has with congressional leaders of both parties. Even more important, presidents can utilize what might be called the social perquisites of their office to ease their relationship with congressmen. President Kennedy overwhelmed some congressmen by inviting them into his office, where they had never been during the Eisenhower years; President Johnson made a point of dancing with the wives of all the congressmen during gala White House evenings. There is no direct relationship between an invitation to waltz and a congressman's vote on a specific matter, but the president can create a climate in which congressmen feel that they are regarded as important members of a governmental team.

One of the major failings of the Nixon administration has been its poor relations with Congress, and a direct link can be seen between this and the isolation of the president. Senator John Sherman Cooper, one of the sponsors of the Cooper-Church Amendment discussed before, was unable to get in to see the president in order to attempt a reconciliation of their differences before the Senate voted. Other Republicans in Congress have complained that they simply cannot get to see him, with some Republican senators reporting that they have been denied access to the Oval Room for as long as 15 months.[28] One senator who managed to get into the office told his colleagues that the president felt he should not drain his energy talking to them when he could read their comments in the *Congressional Record*.[29] Needless to say, no one with President Nixon's history of congressional service has any reason to believe that the *Record* includes all of a congressman's thinking, or that reading his inserted remarks constitutes an adequate substitute for speaking with him. In response to some of the congressional complaints about presidential inaccessibility, the White House scheduled a series of presidential trips down the Potomac on the presidential yacht to be taken in the company of selected congressmen. President Nixon simply did not show up for the trips which were eventually cancelled.[30]

The president has held himself so remote from Congress that Republican congressmen looking to the White House for leadership have been unable to learn how the president wished them to vote on various bills. The Democratic leadership of Congress has been largely ignored in its attempts to establish a working relationship with the president. Again responding to criticism from without and to the necessities of the 1972 campaign, the president after two years in office finally demoted his unsuccessful adviser on congressional relations and appointed a former congressman in his place. The new appointee, Clark MacGregor, was given direct access to the president, and it is possible that this move will be found to have improved the relationship between the two branches of government. There is cause for wonder, however, in one of Mr. MacGregor's first actions which was to order for his fellow presidential aides a supply of lapel buttons reading "I care about Congress."[31]

Congress has begun to discover that the Nixon administration is withholding substantive as well as procedural information. While the administration reported regularly to the North Atlantic Treaty Council on the progress of the United States-Soviet Union negotiations on arms limitations, it refused to brief the Senate Foreign Relations Committee.[32] Senator Stuart Symington's subcommittee on American Security Agreements and Commitments Abroad suddenly discovered late in 1969 that the Eisenhower, Kennedy, Johnson, and Nixon administrations had pledged to "instantly repel" any armed attack on the Philippines, completely bypassing the treaty-making process, and had not bothered to inform the Congress of what had been done.[33] Senator J. W. Fulbright discovered in 1970 that the Nixon administration planned to bypass the treaty-making process once again in signing an agreement with Spain in which each country pledged to "support the defense systems" of the other. When the outraged senator announced that he would seek legislative action forcing the executive branch to submit the agreement to the Senate in the form of a treaty, the secretary of state rushed to sign the agreement before Senator Fulbright had time to put his plan into operation.[34] The secretary of state also outraged Senator Fulbright and his Foreign Relations Committee when, returning from a world-wide trip, he broke all precedent by making no attempt to brief the Committee and then denied its request that he go to the Senate for a meeting.[35] In the meantime, Senator Symington's subcommittee had discovered that what it and the public had been told were volunteer forces from Thailand, Korea, and the Philippines fighting in South Vietnam were actually being paid by the United States government.[36] Additionally, the subcommittee uncovered full-scale American participation in a "secret war" in Laos.[37] This involved bombing and the use of napalm by the Air Force and American financial support of third-country military forces fighting in Laos; according to Senator Symington, it also involved "many" American lives and "billions" of dollars.[38] There seems to have been a systematic attempt by the Nixon administration (and by the Johnson administration, the bombing having begun in 1964) to hide the Laotian war from the Congress. The then-ambassador to Laos and later deputy assistant secretary of state testified before the Senate Foreign Relations Committee in 1968, but conveniently omitted mentioning the Air Force bombing.[39] The Symington subcommittee also discovered that the CIA was operating a military-assistance program in Laos and that the United States was operating a secret naval communications center in Morocco.[40]

In August 1970, the Senate unanimously adopted an amendment to the military appropriations bill it was considering, forbidding the expenditure of United States funds to pay allied troops fighting in Vietnam higher allowances than those paid to American servicemen. Senator Fulbright, the sponsor of the amendment, offered it after Senator Symington's subcommittee discovered that allied troops were being paid approximately twice as much to fight in Vietnam as were American troops. According to Fulbright, it took the subcommittee six months to get the information from the Defense Department.[41] Fulbright also accused the department of using inaccurate figures on the reports that it gives to Congress four times a year; in the period of fiscal 1966 through the second quarter of 1970, for example, the subcommittee discovered that the United States gave forces from the Philippines $40.8 million. The Defense Department had told the Congress that the figure was $17.3 million.[42] Clearly, information has been withheld about those programs for which the Senate votes, and the example cited above is far from the only relevant instance. Senator Symington cites the testimony before the Senate of the director of Defense Research and Engineering who stated that the ABM system would provide the country with all the protection that the Pentagon claimed. The director based his statement on the "O'Neill Report" given to the secretary of defense by a panel of independent scientists. He could not give details, however, because the report was classified. Two members of the panel that had written the report promptly denied that the report contained the conclusions reported by the director, but once again the details could not be given because of security. The Senate thus had to decide whether the ABM would do what it was supposed to without access to the scientific evidence.[43]

More recently, the administration has done its best to withhold information about American involvement in Cambodia from the Senate. The under-secretary of state for political affairs has denied before the Foreign Relations Committee that the United States has any commitment to defend Cambodia in general and the Lon Nol (post-Sihanouk) government in particular.[44] At the same time, it has been a matter of common knowledge among newsmen that the administration has conducted extensive air operations over Cambodia, provided it with millions of dollars worth of military materiel, begun mapping a program of economic aid designed to shore up the Lon Nol government, and sent Vice-President Agnew to Cambodia to pledge publicly that the United States would do "everything we can" for the Lon Nol government.[45] Small wonder that relations between the committee and the administration are severely strained!

The Nixon administration is obviously not the first administration to withhold important information about foreign affairs from the Congress, or to assume that the Senate has no rightful role to play. One commentator reports that in 1965 the Senate was asked to ratify only five treaties while the administration signed 242 executive agreements[46] (which of course do not require Senate ratification but may be as substantively significant as treaties). Louis Heren reports that President Johnson decided not to inform Congress or the public or to seek their support in 1965 when he stepped up the air war in South Vietnam and began extensive bombing of the North because "he was determined to pursue the war with as little debate as possible."[47] This attitude has become a constant source of friction between the two branches. What is new is the systematic downgrading of the Foreign Relations Committee and the administration's unwillingness to work with Congress on problems of domestic policy. The Nixon administration appears to have from the start succumbed to the disease that affected the Johnson adminstration in its last days; namely, the belief that the executive is the only able, informed, suprapolitical branch of the government and that the Congress is an unfortunate, hostile nuisance.

In truth, Congress is sometimes just that. Congress occasionally does create legislative roadblocks out of what seems to be no more than a desire to play up its own importance; Congress is the focus for political pressures of all kinds. Congress, however, is also the major watchdog of the president and an important barometer of public opinion. A president who isolates himself from the Congress in foreign affairs is likely to amass a dangerous concentration of power (even worse, he may be creating the concentration in a highly nonresponsive bureaucracy) while cutting off a guide to popular feeling; a president who isolates himself from the Congress in domestic affairs may find himself ignoring public opinion and will certainly be unable to give the country the social and economic legislation it requires. At the same time, such a president will minimize the already limited popular control over his office as well as his own tactical and legislative power. He will not render the government inoperative, for the bureaucracy keeps the wheels turning no matter what happens at the top of the hierarchy, but he will render it unresponsive to the needs and desires of the country.

6

The Isolation of the Presidency: Press and Public

The Press

The president may surround himself with a small circle of advisers, screen the ideas of his cabinet members, and effectively isolate himself from Congress, but the one outside force he cannot escape is the press. The White House press corps, consisting of the individuals whose only assignment is to follow the president and his staff and file stories about them, has insisted since President Kennedy's death that they be told where the president is at every moment. Usually, when he is outside the White House, they are with him. There is always a press car or bus or plane following the one occupied by the president. At the White House, the press corps works and lounges in a newly refurbished section especially set aside, and it receives at least daily (and often twice-daily) briefings from the presidential press secretary. There are 1,200 or so members of the Washington press corps, all with their own high, medium, and low-level sources of official information, and all competing with each other for the first hint of a news story. Given the tremendous press interest in the president as a personality, as a strategist, and as a political actor, it would be natural to assume that the media function as barriers to those forces tending to isolate the president. Unfortunately, appearances can be deceiving.

Vice-President Agnew's much-publicized attacks on the "liberal" media are ironic when one considers that television is probably the medium with the greatest impact on the public and that the amount of political commentary available on television is minimal. Commentators like David Brinkley allot most of their programs to rehashing the news already reported during the preceding half-hour; or like Eric Sevareid, compress their editorial comments into a few final moments. The occasional special news programs which deal with political issues are usually assigned time slots calculated to attract the fewest possible viewers. Truly insightful reporters about the Washington scene—Tom Wicker, John Osborne, Richard Rovere, Mary McGrory, etc.—confine their efforts almost entirely to the written word, and there are many localities that have regular access to no such commentators. Still, a good deal of commentary concerning the way the president is doing his job can be gathered from the way in which news stories are reported and from columns and editorials in various newspapers and magazines. President Kennedy read avidly and frequently commented to aides about particular articles. Schlesinger claims that no president with the possible exception of Franklin Roosevelt read more newspapers than Kennedy;[1] in any event, each day he read or skimmed the three Washington newspapers; at least three New York City newspapers; two Boston newspapers; two Chicago newspapers; at least one newspaper each from Baltimore, Miami, Philadelphia, and St. Louis; a large number of American periodicals, including both news magazines and journals of opinion; and a number of British newspapers and journals.[2] He also watched the Sunday political panel shows on television.[3] President Johnson added his own twist to a president's constant search for information from the outside world by installing a three-screened console which was never permitted to get cold and two ticker tape machines which constantly tapped out the wire services' latest stories. In addition, he skimmed the *Washington Post, New York Times, Baltimore Sun, Wall Street Journal,* and *Christian Science Monitor;* looked at a special daily annotated *Congressional Record;* listened to news on the radio; and watched the televised "Today" show regularly.[4] One of President Nixon's first acts was to remove his predecessor's television console and ticker tape machines. In an apparent effort to manage his time, he has decided to eliminate direct exposure to the media and to have his news and commentaries predigested. The dangers of this are obvious.

Presidents have held press conferences on a fairly regular basis ever since Woodrow Wilson instituted the custom.[5] Wilson is usually credited with initiating the press conference, although President Theodore Roosevelt held casual question-and-answer sessions with a small group of newsmen while he was being shaved. Quite aside from Wilson's desire to utilize the press conference as a means of letting the public in on the "pitiless publicity" he planned to give the government process, it is difficult to imagine that rather cold, dignified figure inviting reporters to watch a barber slapping shaving cream on his face. But although Wilson may have managed to have meetings with newsmen while preserving his privacy, other problems inherent in the idea of a press conference quickly became apparent. Wilson had certain things he wanted to communicate to the press, and through it, to the electorate, but these were not necessarily the same things the members of the press wanted to know. He was angered by their insistence on asking questions before he was ready to answer them. This is the heart of the problem: the president sees the conference as a method of achieving publicity for his thoughts and ideas, but the press sees the conference as a method of finding out those facts which are not otherwise available to them.

While both are agreed that the conference should be devoted to the president's furnishing information, they are in sharp disagreement about what information should be revealed. Presidents Harding, Coolidge, and Hoover all found the conference format difficult and downgraded it, requiring questions to be submitted in advance.[6]

Press conferences were elevated to an impressive height by President Franklin Roosevelt, who held an astonishing 337 during his first term and 374 during his second.[7] He invited the reporters into his office (according to Schlesinger, there were often more than 100 reporters squeezed into the Oval Office) for a wide-ranging, free-swinging session. He insured the existence of a well-informed press corps by giving them information he was not ready to have circulated among the general public in the form of off-the-record comments and "background" briefings. His example encouraged members of the bureaucracy to hold conferences of their own, the end result being the ability of the "fourth branch" (the press) to act as an informed watchdog.[8] The famous Roosevelt charm apparently worked on the members of the press and he had the satisfaction of seeing his point of view reflected in a good many articles. More important for our purposes was the two-way flow, with Roosevelt learning from the press what issues it (and, presumably, the public) were concerned about and where they hoped he would take action.

President Harry Truman moved the constantly expanding press corps to the treaty room in the old State Department building for his conferences. The move had psychological ramifications. The reporters, who were now assembled before the president's arrival rather than ushered into his office, had to rise to their feet when he entered and wait for his word to be seated; then they returned to their rows of steel folding chairs, only to arise once again and identify themselves when ready to ask a question. The president stood at a desk and the informality of the Roosevelt conferences was lost. Even worse, Truman's propensity for putting his foot in his mouth during news conferences and then to issuing "clarifications" of his remarks turned the conferences into a serious liability for him.

President Dwight Eisenhower further transformed the conferences by allowing them to be recorded on videotape and transmitted to the public after minor editing. The president no longer talked to the reporters, although it was still their questions that he was nominally answering; he now spoke to the television audience. In addition, a stenographer was hired to produce a transcript of each conference, which is regularly reprinted in the *New York Times*. Presidential "clarifications" became more difficult because the president could no longer claim that a reporter had misquoted him. The impact of television on the presidency can be measured by the necessity that President Eisenhower felt to rely on an actor as his television consultant. More than newly acquired television techniques separated president from press: Eisenhower's ability to clothe any question in a vague, rambling answer, often made his news conferences rather unnewsworthy.

The press conference changed once again with President Kennedy and the advent of live television coverage. Kennedy's conferences were frequently good theatre, placing a premium on his highly retentive memory, poise, and wit. Nonetheless, they did not represent simple exchanges between the president and the press. The conferences were moved to the State Department auditorium in order to accommodate the 300 or so newsmen, television technicians, lighting equipment, cameras, cables, etc. Preconference briefing sessions were arranged for the president so that his assistants could warn him of the questions newsmen were most likely to ask and help him to organize the data that would go into his replies. The conferences thus became even more formal and further removed from the spontaneous give-and-take of the Roosevelt years. They also became far less frequent, with President Kennedy averaging 21 conferences a year.[9]

If a president who excelled in his ability to successfully face a huge group of newsmen reduced the number of press conferences he held and thereby indicated his doubts about their usefulness to him, it is not surprising that a president who much preferred face-to-face encounters with individuals and small groups to mammoth formal meetings would indicate his discomfort at their institutionalization. This was the case with President Johnson, who tried half a dozen different locations for his press conferences—his office, his press secretary's office, the White House East Room, the State Department's international conference room, the cabinet room, the LBJ ranch—without really finding one that suited him. President Kennedy had made a practice of beginning conferences with short statements (a clear sign that he saw conferences as a medium for conveying the news that he wanted conveyed); President Johnson both lengthened the opening statements considerably and answered questions with slow, measured replies, thus cutting down the number of questions. His conferences were infrequent, but he did manage to see newsmen singly and in small groups for off-the-record and background briefings, especially in the early years of his presidency.

Anyone elected to the presidency in 1968 would have had to confront Johnson's legacy of a credibility gap and a poor relationship with the press who had become increasingly hostile to his policies. It is ironic that the man in this situation was Richard Nixon, whose own poor relations with the press may have helped to defeat him in 1960[10] and who had culminated his running war with the reporters by telling them furiously in 1962 that now that he had lost the election for governor of California and was leaving public life "You won't have Nixon to kick around anymore."[11] One of the few differences between the Nixon of 1962 and the "new" Nixon of 1968 had been his later ability to meet the press with a cool, pleasant poise. His new style was immediately translated into press conference terms. He did away with the lectern which Lyndon Johnson had fumbled over while searching for data with which to support his replies. The new president strode into his first press conference with no notes in his hand and stepped unencumbered before a microphone. The image conveyed was that of an informed president, sufficiently sure of himself and his policies to face the press without a barricade.

If the impact that the enlarged press corps and improved technology have made on the press conference is to be evaluated, one has only to watch one of President Nixon's conferences. The camera first shows the assembled newsmen and newswomen, packed into neat rows of chairs, chatting among themselves. There is a great hustle and bustle as cameras are rearranged and refocused. Suddenly, the president strides in from an antechamber; the press corps straggles to its collective feet; cameras click madly. Occasionally, the attentive viewer can get a glimpse of a newspaper photographer taking a picture of "president and television cameras" while the television camera focuses on "president and newspaper photographer," which only adds to the surrealistic atmosphere sometimes enveloping press conferences. The president reaches the front of the room, turns, invites the press to be seated. The press corps becomes an undifferentiated mass of television-blue shirt fronts from which different faces will rise to the momentary prominence of question man. The president calls on the first reporter (the representatives of the wire services traditionally ask the first two questions) and the conference is under way.

One man, standing quite alone, facing an array of faces, pencils, cameras, and, beyond, the world. No matter who the president or what the viewer's feelings, one finds oneself silently cheering the underdog and hoping that he will not falter. It is the natural psychological reaction and, as the ensuing conference indicates, it bears no relationship to the facts. This is the president's conference. He has called it, at a time and place of his choosing, and it is only he who will benefit from it.

The president answers the first question, speaking fairly rapidly, clearly, in moderate tones, occasionally chopping his hand through a gesture before returning it to its position behind his back. He looks directly at his questioner (unless he has made a mild joke, at which point he may smile and look around briefly for applause), until he is a few words away from the end of his reply. At that point he quickly swivels his head and turns his gaze to the other side of the room. The last word is spoken; he immediately recognizes another reporter.

The implication of the turned head is that the first reporter has had his chance and now it is time for somebody else. No one is going to say to the president of the United States, in front of the whole world "No, don't turn away, you haven't really answered my question." Here lies the flaw that renders the press conference almost undistinguishable from a series of White House hand-outs; no reporter is permitted to follow up his question. The president may reply with meaningless platitudes, or twist the question until he is answering his own rather than the reporter's, and there is nothing the newsman can do about it. There it is, the president's official reply, and that's all the information on the subject that the conference is likely to produce.

More information might well emerge if the next questioner was willing to forego his planned question to follow up on the preceding one. This rarely happens, largely because each reporter wants to see how much he can learn about the particular subject that interests him and he knows he will have only one brief chance at the conference. There are enough subjects of political importance on any one day to ensure the probability of no two questions on the same aspect of the same subject. Thus the president can hold his conference, accept the applause of the electorate for having performed his duty, and divest himself only of that information that he was prepared to make public anyway.

Any conference provides a plethora of examples. Let us turn to the conference held on July 30, 1970, selected purely at random (any other conference would yield precisely the same result). A sample:

Q. Mr. President, the Wholesale Price Index registered in July its greatest gain in six months. Can you tell us when you expect prices to go down?
A. What I am more interested in is, of course, not just what happens in one month but what happens over the six-month period. And what we are encouraged by is the fact that the trend in the six-month period for wholesale prices was downward; the rise of the rate of increase is downward rather than upward.
This three-tenth of a percent increase to which you refer has to be balanced against a zero increase in the month of May. The zero increase in the month of May does not mean the rise in wholesale prices could stop, just as this does not mean that a rise in wholesale prices will escalate.
We believe, based on not only wholesale prices but other economic indicators, that the inflation is being cooled, that it will continue to be cooled if we can continue to have responsibility in the conduct of our budget problems in Washington, D.C., and that we are on the way, so far as the other side of the coin is concerned, with an economy moving upward in the last-half (sic) of 1970.[12]

The president's reply is reprinted in its entirety. It would be instructive to stop for a moment and consider what is now known about the president's expectations vis-a-vis lower prices that was not known before the answer was delivered. The president has said that the *trend* of prices has been *to move upward more slowly* than the prices had risen during an earlier period; the best he can point to is the month of May, when prices neither rose nor fell. "We believe" (notice the impressive anonymity of that "we"—it conjures up a vision of crowds of learned economists standing firmly behind the president) that inflation is slowing down (no figures or proof given) and that the economy will move upward in the next few months (why this should lead to lower rather than higher prices, or whether the president really thinks it will, is left unclear). When will prices go down? Nobody knows. The president has spoken with confidence and a sincere mien; he has quoted statistics; he has not answered the question.

Or take Question 14 (the questions which evoked the shortest answers are reprinted here because of space limitations; examination of the lengthy answers to the other questions indicate that increased length is not an indication of increased substance.):

Q. Mr. President, do you see any improvement in the objectivity and fairness of the nation's press in light of the statements by the vice-president about the press?

A. Well, my reaction is that I recall once having comments about the press in California when I was here, and that didn't seem to get me very far. All I can say now is: I just wish I had as good a press as my wife has, and I'd be satisfied.[13]

Everyone had a hearty laugh at the president's reference to his 1962 remarks and the president went on to the next question. The important matter of the relationship between the vice-president and the press he had accused of proliberal antiadministration bias went undiscussed.

Q. Mr. President, a few days ago some organization—Mexican-American organizations—called on you for 55,000 jobs in the federal government. Have you anything to comment on that?
A. Yes. We have provided more opportunities for Mexican-Americans than any administration in history. It is of high priority for this administration. As you know, Mr. Castigal from Los Angeles is working with us in the White House on this proposition.
And, second, we would welcome Mexican-Americans who are qualified, who are interested in government positions—we would welcome them in government positions. We're looking for them, we're just trying to see that they are qualified and we hope they will have the qualifications.[14]

How many people are actually implied in "more opportunities for Mexican-Americans than any administration in history?" Half a dozen? Tens? Hundreds? Thousands? Does the president consider 55,000 an unrealistic goal? an undesirable goal? Does he think numerical goals should be set for specific ethnic groups? What does "qualified" mean in this context? Does it imply the possession of skills with which the nation's schools are not currently equipping the majority of Mexican-Americans? Will the administration consider altering the usual qualifications required for civil service positions? If not, will it encourage or undertake remedial work designed to help those "who are interested in government positions" to attain the qualifications? The fact that the federal government does not have an official policy of discriminating against Mexican-Americans who can pass civil service examinations was never in doubt. No other concrete information on the subject was proffered.

Two important points were made during the press conference. One involved the solidity of American support for Israel (Question 1), the other the determination of the Nixon administration to seek limitations on the arms race that would not imply the United States' falling behind in military preparedness. The Egyptian and Jordanian acceptance of the United States' cease fire proposal earlier in the week and the statements of high-ranking naval officers during the preceding days made questions on the two topics inevitable. His answers indicate that the president had something he wanted to say about each and came prepared to do so. The information he wanted to convey was conveyed; information he was not prepared to yield was not obtained.

It is the president who calls on reporters during the conference. He knows their names, what their interests are, and their probable points of view. He can choose his questioners on this basis. It has long been taken for granted that all recent presidents have "salted" the press corps with a few reliable reporters who have been primed to ask the questions which the president particularly wants to answer. Sorensen admits that President Kennedy occasionally learned from his press secretary that he could expect a specific question at an upcoming press conference and that on a few occasions the president planted questions.[15] Presidential familiarity with the White House press corps implies another limitation on the usefulness of the press conference: since the corps must rely on the president and his official family for information, no White House reporter is overly eager to push the president too far in public. Worth Bingham and Ward S. Just tell the story of a *Time* magazine White House correspondent who found all of his White House sources cut off for a frightening two weeks after *Time* printed an article which infuriated President Kennedy.[16] The same thing can happen if the president decides that a reporter has been overly rude during a press conference.

Even though the press conference is unlikely to prove a source of surprising news, a president's willingness to submit to conferences is an indication of his willingness to place himself in direct relationship with press and public, if only momentarily.[17] It is instructive to note that, according to President Nixon's press secretary, President Nixon had ten conferences in his first 19 months in office; President Johnson, 14; President Kennedy, 38. President Nixon appeared on television for a total of 13 hours, 32 minutes; President Johnson, 12 hours, 38 minutes; President Kennedy, 30 hours, 16 minutes.[18]

The president's major contacts with the press may take place in the relative anonymity of the White House. President Kennedy had certain favorite newsmen to whom he granted exclusive interviews and "leaked" information, among them Marquis Childs, Joseph and Stewart Alsop, Charles Bartlett, and perhaps a dozen or so more.[19] After initial and unsuccessful attempts to woo the entire presidential press corps,[20] President Johnson confined his private information-granting to such trusted press friends as William S. White.[21] Those newsmen who Johnson continued to trust were carefully cultivated and became privy to a good deal of presidential thinking. This remained true throughout the Johnson administration; even after he reduced his public meetings with the press, beginning in 1966, he continued to see certain correspondents privately. The important point is that some newsmen were getting into the Oval Office, especially during the Kennedy administration, and that this "selective open door" attitude began to permeate the higher echelons of the bureaucracy who began to open *their* doors.[22] The net result was a flow of news and a partial break in presidential isolation.

There seems to be no similar relationship with newsmen in the Nixon administration; although a few columnists have been granted private talks, President Nixon's dealings with the press have been primarily the formal ones of press secretary briefings and large-scale press conferences. He has virtually abolished individual interviews with members of the press.[23] Whereas President

Johnson met with the White House press corps informally on an average of 18 times a week as of August 1970, President Nixon had done so twice.[24] In addition, the president has adopted the strategy, reportedly devised by Herbert Klein,[25] of circumventing the newsmen entirely by dealing only with their editors and publishers. He has held a series of "backgrounders" (which means that he and Henry Kissinger, who appears regularly at the sessions, cannot be quoted, and so the public cannot learn what they said) for media executives from various sections of the country.[26] He thus assures himself of a far friendlier reception that he can expect from the White House press corps. When he deals with individual newspapers, he makes sure they are friendly. He granted an exclusive conference to the editors of the friendly *Washington Star*, but not to those of the critical *Washington Post*; as well as one to the sympathetic *New York Daily News*, but not to the critical *New York Times* or *New York Post*.

One president-watcher has called Nixon "the most inaccessible President since Herbert Hoover."[27] Another points out that in moving the White House press corps from the West Lobby into its far more comfortable present quarters on the spot of the former White House swimming pool, Nixon also moved them to where they can no longer see who goes in and out of the Oval Office.[28] The same commentator notes that President Nixon appears to have ordered a "rule of reticence" for those who work in the White House[29] and that he has become "the hidden president."[30] Robert B. Semple, Jr. has labeled him "an exceptionally private man."[31] His attitude toward the working press permeates his administration. Secretary of State Rusk, for example, held regular sessions almost every Friday evening with the newsmen who covered the State Department; Secretary Rogers has discontinued this practice.[32]

It should be noted, however, that even those presidents who are more accessible to individual newsmen do not end the isolation problem. The very relationship which enables them to share their thinking with certain reporters necessarily affects the objectivity of the newsmen. The reporters may develop close personal ties to the president, which clearly makes their reporting more subjective; even if they do not, their fear of cutting off their exclusive source is bound to make them cautious about printing critical statements or asking searching questions. Even President Nixon admits that Washington is somewhat isolated intellectually from the rest of the country and is experimenting with taking the White House to the people. The ability of the similarly isolated Washington press corps and particularly the White House press corps to perceive the questions that need to be asked may be somewhat impaired. They too may become so involved in the convolutions of Washington politics and personnel that they forget to scrutinize policies for their moral and practical implications.

Every recent president has had a press secretary whose job is to brief newsmen on a regular basis. The secretary is the president's press secretary, which is merely another way of saying that his primary loyalty must be to the president rather than to the press corps. He saves the president the time it takes to speak with the reporters, but he says only those things that the president wants said. He hardly represents a crack in the wall surrounding the chief executive; neither does the director of communications for the executive branch, a post created by President Nixon for Herbert Klein. Although the duty of the director was heralded as opening up government to the reporters, who had complained of the Johnson credibility and information gaps, Klein has functioned as just another press secretary, with the broader job of coordinating the information released by the entire executive branch. He has also become yet another of the many watchdogs who stand between the presidency and the outside world.

It is possible that the extreme formality in the relationship between the president and the press is at least in part responsible for another element in presidential isolation. Both president and press in the United States tend to define the job of the press as solely reporting about the president to the people and not at all as reporting about the people to the president. This means that even a president who maximizes his availability to the press may convey additional information and respond to the professional and personal curiosity of the press corps, but he will still not learn much about the concerns of the rest of the electorate.

Thus the existence of the large, aggressive, intelligent, and highly skilled press corps does not necessarily imply the ability of the electorate to find out what is going on in the White House, nor does it imply presidential awareness of the major concerns of the country at large. There is one more link between president and public: the public itself.

The Public

Anyone who wants to can sit down and write a letter to the president. No matter how incorrectly addressed it may be, it has an excellent chance of reaching the White House. But what happens to it then?

It has already been mentioned that the presidential mail is cross-indexed and abstracted for President Nixon. In spite of his skepticism about the representative nature of presidential mail, President Kennedy went further and read every fiftieth letter that arrived at the White House.[33] It would be difficult for President Nixon to do this: while President Kennedy averaged 30,000 letters a week,[34] the White House received up to 80,000 letters a day immediately following the Cambodian invasion and the deaths of the Kent State students in the spring of 1970.[35] Telephone calls and telegrams from citizens are also received at the White House, especially after an important event or a major presidential television appearance. Presidents are wont to boast about the support for their policies as reflected in their mail; it therefore becomes germane to ask who it is that writes to the president.

Interest groups often undertake letter-writing campaigns, sometimes going so far as to print political postcards for distribution to their members, who have only to sign their names and addresses. School children may write as part of a civics project, retired people, housewives, and others with some time to spare, those interested in particular problems but not allied with a pressure group, cranks, the civic-minded, etc.[36] However, most Americans have probably never written to any government official and know no one who has. The question that obviously arises is what kind of cross-sample can be obtained from these letters, and how representative is that sample? When the White House takes a hand in soliciting its own mail, the question becomes all the more significant.

In November 1969, President Nixon appealed on television for the "silent majority" to communicate to him its support of his Vietnam policy. The result was 310,000 letters, running 2½ to 1 in support of the policy.[37] When President Nixon made the final decision to invade Cambodia, Charles W. Colson, the president's special counsel in charge of special interest group liaison, immediately mobilized his associates to telephone Republicans and interest groups to ask them to indicate their support. The immediate result was a myriad of telephone calls and telegrams applauding the president's action.[38] The outpouring in both instances was completely misleading if interpreted as an indication that an overwhelming majority of voters stood behind the president. As will be indicated later, support for the president's Vietnam policy was far from overwhelming; of the letters that poured into the White House after Cambodia, something between 50 and 60 percent approved of the action.[39] Since people tend to write to those officials whose policies please them, the presidential mail may be lopsided. Immediately after Cambodia, Senator Fulbright's mail, which numbered into hundreds of thousands of communications (letters, telegrams, petitions, etc.), reflected 97 percent support of his adamant opposition to the invasion.[40]

There is also the matter of who is doing the counting. Clayton Fritchey, political columnist of the *New York Post,* reported that the Chairman of the Department of Religion at Wesleyan University telephoned the White House after Cambodia to express an opinion. He was asked which side he favored and when he said he opposed the invasion the telephone line went dead. Apparently in an experimental mood, the professor called back and said he wished to be recorded in support of the action. The operator promptly asked how many members there were in his family and counted them all as votes in favor of invasion.[41]

The public can also express itself on the issues of the day by writing letters to local newspapers. While the letters to the editor column of most newspapers may constitute an outlet for some who do not write directly to the president, the columns are not necessarily representative of the electorate. One may speculate that it is the more literate members of society who choose to write; certainly, it is they who read such columns, and it is doubtful that this includes the majority of Americans. Additionally, those letters which are printed represent a choice on the part of the editors. The choice may be made on literary or amusement grounds, or because subjects have not been previously covered in the column, or because of the profession of the writer. These are all matters of legitimate concern to editors, none of which guarantees either a balanced presentation of views or a reflection of the number of readers holding each opinion.

Finally, there are public opinion polls. President Johnson always seemed to have one handy, ready to be waved in the faces of his detractors. Although his aides rely on them, President Nixon is reported to be far more skeptical about the meaning of polls than was his predecessor.[42] The skepticism is warranted, given such problems as the limited number of topics covered by polls, the selection of respondents, the limited choice of possible answers, the unconscious desire of respondents to select the answer wanted by the pollster, etc. Thus, polls probably do little to diminish the isolation of the presidency.

President or King?

George E. Reedy, who served President Johnson as press secretary and special assistant, has argued that the presidency as an institution is not applicable to the needs of a twentieth century democratic state.[43] Reedy asserts that the presidency has been converted into a nonhereditary monarchy, surrounded by all the panoply associated with kings and tolerating no real dissent within the court. He sees the combination of the offices of chief of state and chief executive in the same man as undercutting the chief executive's ability to maintain touch with reality.

What happens to the ego of a man who occupies the White House? Consider the following: President and Mrs. Kennedy decided that formal dinners at the White House should be accompanied by continuous music. For that purpose, they had at their command the Marine band (which the president ordered to be outfitted in brilliant red coats), the Drum and Bugle Corps, the Air Force Strolling Strings, the Sea Chanters, the Army Chorus, and other assorted musical groups. When they wanted more sophisticated entertainment, they summoned the stars and/or cast of Broadway hits, who promptly canceled performances in order to appear in Washington for command performances. Nobel Prize winners flocked to the White House for dinners and performances of chamber music. When the Kennedys entertained President Mohammed Ayub Khan of Pakistan, four yachts conveyed guests to a state dinner at Mount Vernon. Marines in full dress uniform lined the road from the landing pier to the mansion, which the guests traveled in Cadillacs. The mansion and grounds were spotlighted with special electric lights. No unwanted insects were attracted by the lights, for Army engineers had spent three days spraying the area for four square miles around. Guests were seated at small tables in a tent (the electric lights installed elsewhere were foregone in the tent, which was lighted by candles). René Verdon, the French chef installed in the White House by the Kennedys, cooked the dinner in the White House and a fleet of mobile Army field kitchens carried it to Mount Vernon. Afterdinner entertainment consisted of a concert by the National Symphony, champagne, Corona Corona cigars, and dancing on the yachts.[44] As Heren says, Kennedy "frankly enjoyed the monarchical side of the presidency."[45]

President Nixon has continued the ceremonial tradition. When White House dinner guests are assembled, Marine buglers begin the formal proceedings with a fanfare played on their banner-draped horns. The Marine band then plays processional music while President and Mrs. Nixon walk down the staircase and into the East Room. Their entrance into the East Room itself is greeted with "Ruffles and Flourishes" and "Hail to the Chief." The route to the state dining room is lined with military aides standing at attention. Once inside, hosts and guests are served by waiters in impeccable white gloves. And when the Nixons decide that the party is over, the Marine band again blares out a march while the president and his wife ascend the staircase.[46] All of this is besides the usual retinue of butlers, maids, gardeners, etc., that make White House living well-orchestrated comfort, and the retinue is growing. In the summer of 1970, the president added three Marines to White House duty. The sole function of what the president envisioned as his "honor guard" was to stand in fulldress uniform outside the entrance to the West Wing and open car doors and the building door whenever necessary.[47]

The pageantry and super service continue outside the White House. President Nixon visited New York in August 1970 and at one point decided to take an impromptu walk down Fifth Avenue. He gave the police virtually no notice; nevertheless, he was surrounded during his little stroll by an estimated 30 uniformed policemen and 20 Secret Servicemen and detectives.[48] When the President chooses to travel outside the country, every step of the way is paved for him. Air Force One, the primary presidential plane, makes one or two trial runs whenever the president plans to land at a foreign airport.[49] His every possible stopping place is readied by an army of aides. Both mansions owned by an Irish-American millionaire contributor to the Republican Party were prepared for a presidential stay when the president journeyed to Ireland. He decided to stay in one rather than the other, so the second Army Signal Corps switch-board with its operators, technicians, and newly installed miles of telephone wire had to be dismantled without ever having been used.[50]

Without denying that the president and his family ought to live in comfort, it is possible to wonder whether the kind of everyday existence led behind the walls of the White House is conducive to an understanding of the forces that are raging beyond. Even President Nixon, who is described by the *New York Times* as being dominated by "a passion for order and a passion for solitude,"[51] has admitted that "those at the highest level are like in an isolation booth in the old quiz shows, where the man inside cannot hear what's going on outside."[52] As Reedy suggests, it would be difficult for a man isolated from the outside world and treated like an infallible monarch within his own castle not to begin thinking of himself as more than mortal. His surroundings and his aides are constant reminders of his uniqueness: he is the only president the country has, as Lyndon Johnson was wont to observe; he is the only American making the hard decisions; he must be coddled and obeyed and protected. His time is more important than anyone else's; his desires must always take precedence.

The harsh light of reality is not far away. It is as near as Capitol Hill, or even as close as a television set—*if* the president listens to congressmen or watches anything but sports events. The point is that if a man has any tendencies at all toward believing that he can handle anything if only the world will leave him alone,[53] they are bound to be encouraged while he occupies the office of the president.

7

Social Justice
and the President's
View of His Role

The preceding chapters have examined the extent to which a president can isolate himself from his own government and from the people, and suggested that such isolation has almost been built into the modern presidency. The isolation can only be avoided if a president is constantly determined to avoid it. This raises the problem of what kind of president under what circumstances can be expected to seek maximum communication with the world outside the White House. This, in turn, leads to the problem of the president's view of his role.

There is a direct correlation between the president's willingness to isolate himself and the way in which he views his role. It is usual to hear various presidents described as "strong" or "weak," meaning that "strong" presidents have a positive, dynamic view and hence take steps to place themselves in the midst of all important political activity, whereas "weak" presidents have a negative, passive view of their office and tend to leave the politicking and policy formulation to others.[1] Thus President Eisenhower, who began his tenure with the assumption that his function was to be essentially apolitical and aloof from the passions of the day, quite logically saw no need to remain in close touch with the people or to engage in a struggle for power with Congress. President Kennedy, with his idea that the presidency was "where the power is" and his deep desire to put his imprint on the course of American politics, concentrated on information-gathering and inevitably collided with Congress. If one looks at the presidential career of Richard Nixon, however, one discovers that the traditional strong-weak dichotomy does not shed sufficient light on presidential tendencies toward isolation.

Most of the modern "strong" presidents—Wilson, Roosevelt, possibly

Truman, Kennedy, Johnson—have had a tremendous zest for power. They fought long and hard for power and for the presidency (or for the positions that were to catapult them into the presidency) and once having achieved the office, relinquished power only reluctantly. The distinguishing characteristic of the modern "strong" president has been his belief in the valid use of political power as a means to a specific end. Each of these presidents came to the office equipped with a vision of the optimum American society and a determination to utilize the power of the government to achieve it. While they may have been uncertain as to details, they had an overall view which enabled them to insist that they knew what was right for the political system. Clemenceau is reported to have commented that "Talking to Wilson is like talking to Jesus Christ";[2] certainly, Wilson was insistent that only his view of American society, and indeed the world, was acceptable. The labels that historians have given to recent administrations—New Deal, Fair Deal, New Frontier, Great Society—reflect the specific vision of past presidents. The mark of the strong president is the recognition that his vision cannot be achieved without deft manipulation of the existing political machinery. Theodore Roosevelt said "I believe in a strong executive. I believe in power." President Eisenhower, the model of a weak president, told a press conference, "In the general derogatory sense you can say that, of course, I do not like politics."[3] A man who dislikes the struggle for power that constitutes the essence of politics obviously cannot be a strong president, since the goals of any president cannot be achieved without much political battling.

It would seem logical, therefore, that those presidents who fought hard for their jobs, enjoy power, and see the president as a political figure, would be those who would surmount the isolating tendencies of the White House. No good general attempts to fight a battle without sufficient information; no good politician makes any significant move without first gauging his chances of success. The record does show that the dynamic presidents have sought to maximize their sources of information. FDR set aides against each other in an attempt to hear the best from both sides and sent a corps of "eyes and ears," including his wife, to sound out opinion in the country. Truman set aside periods of the day for hearing citizens' complaints, and, on one occasion, sent a friendly Secretary of the Senate to the Midwest disguised as a farmer in order to ascertain the feelings of the agricultural community.[4] Kennedy read widely and sought those in touch with different segments of the electorate. Johnson, during his early presidency, required a constant flow of information about the desires of all of his constituents in order to achieve the politics of consensus. The later and more embittered Johnson, ignored his earlier pattern, completely isolated himself from the people, and turned the White House into "a beleagured frontier fort in Indian country."[5] Lyndon Johnson in 1967 and 1968 still enjoyed the exercise of power; he still possessed his vision of the Great Society. Nonetheless, his communication with much of the country was almost nonexistent. The traditional strong-weak dichotomy is clearly unable to account for this, too.

Richard Nixon seems to have spent most of his adult life running for the presidency. He has suffered setbacks which would have undoubtedly discouraged less determined individuals: public questioning of his ethics, President Eisenhower's unenthusiastic backing, Kennedy's winning the election in 1960, and his losing the California governor's race and subsequent exile in New York. Thus President Nixon fills the first requirement for a strong president: a tremendous desire for power, and specifically, the power of the presidency. And although his uncanny ability to seize the issue of the day and make it his own, has been one of the key factors in his political survival, he does appear to have a specific vision of American society. His vision accepts both the Horatio Alger myth and the necessity for giant corporations as organizing principles in our society; the primacy of regulars in the political world, along with the secondary role accorded to ideology; the importance of politically useful cliches (law, order, discipline, patriotism, the family); and the growing homogeneity of much of the world in the American image, as well as distrust of those nations that do not follow this model. It is a vision of America as white; male, middle-aged, and Anglo-Saxon.

Perhaps President Nixon's vision was a viable one at some point in American history, although the dynamics and ferment of American development makes this unlikely. Nevertheless, it is not a vision which bears much relationship to the realities of the 1970s. Women, blacks, youths, and non-Americans will neither "stay in their places" nor disappear, nor will the poor or the alienated or the political dissenters. The New Deal, the Fair Deal, the New Frontier, and the Great Society all represented visions of a society that had never existed before in American history and that might never be fully achieved but that took advantage of the new possibilities of each historical moment. As Thomas Wolfe put it, you *can't* go home again. The internal logic of history makes it impossible to return to times past and dimly remembered.

Thus there are two major factors which differentiate Nixon's vision of American society from those of other recent "strong" presidents. One is its backward-looking nature; the other is its disregard for social justice. "Social justice" in the American context has come to mean bringing disadvantaged groups into the mainstream of American political and economic life. It will be suggested later that current conditions of life in the United States may require modification of this definition. The definition as it stands, however, represents a phenomenon that has been an important element in American history. The concern for social justice has widened and accelerated since the Great Depression, with attempts to bring the poor, blacks, women, Puerto Ricans, Mexican-Americans, and the American Indians into the mainstream of American life. During the administrations of recent strong presidents, the impetus for social justice revolved in some measure around the White House.

This is not to argue that a president's role is confined to the area of social justice, or that a President's success can be judged solely on the basis of his actions in one area. As has been suggested earlier, the president's role includes such elements as the presentation of a unified legislative program to the Congress, administration of the bureaucracy, education of the public, etc. Other elements which have not been discussed also figure importantly: preparation of the budget, appointment of officials, guidance of the economy, etc. What is argued here is that an increasingly insistent emphasis on social justice has become a constant theme in American politics, and that a president who ignores the problem and adheres to a vision that does not take into account the demands for social justice is bound to be a president whose vision is at least partially irrelevant.

An administration today may not chalk up gains in social justice, but it is highly unlikely that it will see a major regression to an earlier period. The Northern schools that remain segregated, for example, may not move toward integration, but neither will the South revert back to an overt dual public school system. Many black Americans may continue to be unable to afford a meal in a restaurant, but restaurants will not return to a whites-only policy. This kind of stagnation is clearly unacceptable, and the recognition that it may occur is not meant to legitimize it in any way. The important point is that Americans as a whole have assimilated into their political philosophies whatever degree of social justice exists in the United States and that, however bigoted they may be, most Americans would greet with shock and dismay a deliberate attempt to erase (instead of slow down) the gains of the past decades. Thus a president whose vision is either regressive or neutral about social justice has nothing to champion. He can only help to continue the present level of social injustice through absence of presidential leadership, but he can not actively campaign for inequities.

A strong president is by definition a president who fights for and amasses political power in order to effect certain changes in the political system; ergo, a president who has no goals cannot be a strong president. And if one is not going to fight for power, or attempt to alter the body politic, there is no need to put together the kind of information system that will enable one to fight successfully. Obviously, no president is totally disinterested in power, just as no president will find there is nothing he cares enough about to fight for. All presidents appoint federal judges and prepare federal budgets, to take but two examples, and presumably they are willing to do some fighting for their choices. One cannot win a fight without information about both allies and enemies. The need for information of a president who is neutral on social justice issues, however, will be extremely limited, and may prove insufficient to overcome the tendency toward isolation that is built into the modern presidency.

Congress, as was previously indicated, tends to be a conservative body. Its institutional predisposition is against change. A president who is uninterested in change need only leave the political process entirely to the Congress. If he wants no significant changes to occur, he can surely count on the Congress. Thus a president who possesses a vision which is regressive in nature and which ignores the problem of social justice in particular cannot be an active, dynamic president. He will remain powerful, that is, he can prevent others from effecting change; but he will not amass an impressive record of accomplishments for his administration. Should he decide that there are battles which are important to him, he will discover that his isolation has made it unlikely that sporadic attempts to exercise power will succeed. This surely is the lesson of President Nixon's ill-fated Carswell and Haynsworth nominations.

Even a president whose natural inclination is to be far from remote and who perceives that his role includes a commitment to social justice may not be successful in eliminating isolation or in furthering social justice. The example of President Johnson, especially in the last three years of his Administration, is instructive. President Johnson's vision of the United States included universal education as a practical key to social justice. It was he who not only incorporated the phrase "We shall overcome" into a major presidential address and thus helped to legitimize the civil rights movement; it was also Johnson as Majority Leader who guided the forerunners of the 1964 Civil Rights Act through the Senate during the Eisenhower years. His commitment to social justice, which may have resulted from his experiences among the Texas poor and from his debut into national politics at the time of the Depression, was undeniable. The Great Society program, hastily conceived, patched-together, and under-funded though it was, represented an attempt to achieve Johnson's vision. What happened to it, of course, was the war in Vietnam.

From 1966 through the end of his administration, Lyndon Johnson found himself the reputed master of an increasingly divided house. The tempo of antiwar feelings and demonstrations across the country increased, as did the doubts of members of the executive branch. George Christian reports that the antiwar contingent within that branch came to include assistant-secretaries of some departments, public affairs officers, and a few cabinet members.[6] Although congressional disaffection as a whole never reached the heights of the Cooper-Church and Hatfield-McGovern amendments, a large number of senators and a smaller proportion of congressmen had begun to make public their distress over the war. The promise of *both* "butter and guns" began to disappear as the seemingly endless demand for military materiel drained the resources from the Great Society programs. It might be said that Johnson's vision of democracy for Vietnam and the social justice he hoped would ultimately result from democracy (or at least anti-Communism) made the achievement of social justice at home impossible.

Johnson's insistence on fighting the war in Vietnam his way; namely, with increasingly greater infusions of men and money in spite of the fact that the war never came close to victory, led to the much-publicized credibility gap. When Johnson insisted that he retained his commitment to social justice, he was not believed. When he argued that his programs would work if Congress and the public would only give him the time and money necessary, he was not believed. And, indeed, his commitment to the war may have deprived those programs of the continuing evaluation and impetus from the top they required.

Thus Johnson's potential as a strong president was gradually negated by his adherence to a major policy that divided the public and government officials while turning national attention and resources away from social justice programs that Johnson might otherwise have been able to create and implement. Although some hardy individuals attempted to indicate to Johnson that his thinking diverged considerably from that of much of the country, he refused to listen. Hubert Humphrey, his vice-president, has since said that Johnson "was absolutely paranoid about the war ... Beyond his ego, ... you've got to remember he had two sons-in-law who were over there. Why, anybody who said the sllllightest [sic] thing to him about change in Vietnam, why, my Lord ..."[7] What Johnson ignored was the necessity for a rapport with the electorate that is the final hallmark of the strong president.

Recent presidents have tended to view themselves, rather than Congress, as the repository of the public trust. Americans in the early days of the United States considered themselves "Virginians" or "New Yorkers" rather than "Americans"; greater emphasis was put on the power and political predispositions of the government officials responsible to them alone, i.e., their representatives in Congress. After the Civil War made this kind of state-centered parochialism impossible, the Congress nevertheless remained the dominant body in Washington. Domestic affairs, which are the special domain of Congress, were paramount, and the country turned with relief from a period of strong governmental leadership to one of innovation and domination by the economic community. It was not until Theodore Roosevelt took office that the country had a strong, modern president, and after he left office it took two successive national crises—World War I and the Depression—to persuade the country to elect two more strong presidents. The great importance of foreign affairs since World War II, the interaction of foreign and domestic affairs, the technology that shrinks world distances, and the sophisticated communications systems that place presidential addresses and activity before every American, all have led the American public to look to the president rather than to the Congress as a source of leadership and guidance. The practice of listing on the ballot the names of presidential hopefuls rather than the names of the electors for whom the ballot is actually being cast has led Americans to think of the president as a popularly elected figure. He is *our* president; *we* elect him; he is directly responsible to *us*. Thus we have the ideological justification for the exercise of great power: the president is the only nationally elected official; he alone can claim that he acts in the name of the entire electorate.

No president can act with great decisiveness unless he believes this. When congressmen, bureaucrats, interest groups, or even his own advisers argue against his proposals, he must believe that his vision, his sense of social justice, and his unique relationship with the electorate justify his insistence on his own point of view. Were this not the case, the president would become no more than the sum of the majority of his advisers, formal and informal. He must believe that his sense of right is shared by the public, or that although the public does not see his point immediately, they will eventually agree that he is correct. No matter how abundant or brilliant his advisers, it is the president who must make the final decisions. As the sign on Harry Truman's desk reminded everyone, "The buck stops here"; as subsequent presidents must surely constantly remember, so does the final authority to command a nuclear war. Any man who is going to function effectively as a strong president must possess an enormous amount of self-confidence, or, to put it more simply, a large ego.

There is, however, a difference between possessing an ego adequate to the job of president and ignoring the will of the electorate. A president must recognize that, as he is the repository of the collective will, he bears a special responsibility to the public. He must both reflect the national will and lead it, helping to shape it with all the persuasive arts at his command, but he simply must not ignore it. He may believe that he is at one with the American people, but he must continue to make sure that he is not out of touch. Unless he does, he is not only morally reprehensible, but he will be unable to function effectively.

The previous definition of "strong" and "weak" presidents needs to be revised, for it is obvious that any president of the last third of the twentieth century would be considered "strong" in comparison to most of the presidents of an earlier age. Foreign leaders will accord him respect and take his possible reactions into account when formulating their own policies, Congress will turn to him for a comprehensive legislative program and for guidance on specific policies, and the people will assume that he is the one to solve all the serious domestic problems in the country. Whoever he is, he is empowered by statutes that make it impossible for him to refuse to exercise powers upon which any president of the last third of the nineteenth century would surely stand in awe. Today's president must appoint thousands of policy-makers to non civil service jobs; he must respond to the ups and downs of the business cycle and the resulting manpower situation; he must prepare an annual budget which provides for the expenditure of billions of dollars, among a myriad of other responsibilities.

The fact that the president and his advisers prepare the budget each year is important simply because it makes it impossible for anyone but the president to give the American government an organized, comprehensive legislative program. No matter how high taxes are there is always a limit on the amount of money available for governmental activity. A president who includes large appropriations both for development of a supersonic transport plane and for superhighways in one year's budget thereby limits the funds available for a myriad of other activities covered by the budget. The budget is interconnected. It looks like an economic document, but it is a political and social one as well, for the proposed appropriation of federal monies is also a statement of priorities and choices. Congress can cutback funds in some areas or increase the allotments to others; create and fund entirely new programs; require when and in what way federal money is spent; but it cannot control the overall approach to government that is implicit in the annual budget. If during one fiscal year priority must be given to domestic rather than foreign programs, particular aspects of the economy, or the quality rather than the quantity of life, this must be reflected in the budget. The budget as published is a massive document. No congressman or aide has the time or the expertise to plow through it all, so congressmen are forced to confine themselves largely to those features of the budget which are of particular interest to them. Thus there is cutting and adding, but there will never be any unified congressional reorganization of the priorities in the budget. The fact of the budget means that the president is, and will continue to be, the country's chief political figure and the official most responsible for the direction in which the country is moving.

Thus a president who does not lead the country toward social justice will be president of a country which is unable to move toward pervasive social justice. Pressure to exercise such leadership almost always will come from below, as it did during the Kennedy administration, but the leadership can come only from the very top. It must be remembered, however, that the presidency does not include sufficient power to ensure leadership in domestic affairs. The president may be willing to accede to the demands of various groups concerned with social justice, but the public and the congressmen who represent them may not be immediately responsive.

While various statutes do present modern presidents with some power that can be exercised through publication of such documents as the Budget, they do not in themselves constitute sufficient power to govern the nation effectively. President Johnson, who had the drive and ability to amass and utilize power, lost power because he isolated himself from the American people. He continued to greet foreign dignitaries, compile the budget, and send reports on the state of the Union and requests for specific programs to Congress. From 1966 on, appointments were made, the bureaucracy operated as usual, and the machinery of the country functioned. But it did not function particularly well because it was not being governed well. And it was not being governed well because the Chief Governor no longer understood what was going on in the nation.

Similarly, President Nixon continues to exercise power. He too sends messages and makes decisions and the country continues to function. But, deliberately isolated as he is, he cannot possibly understand the nature or the magnitude of the internal problems faced by the nation, and so he does nothing about them. He fought for power, he clearly enjoys the idea of being president, he intends to go on fighting for power, and he is certain that what he does is right. But he is not a strong president. Since he is cut off from the people, he can continue to believe that he embodies their ideals and understands their aspirations while the people turn against each other and tear the fabric of the nation. Power unexercised is not power. The potential ability to get people to do things they would not otherwise do is only potential power. Perhaps Richard Nixon could be a strong president if he tried, but his conception of his role revolves around an aloof president in a status quo society and so there is no reason for him to try.

The communication between any president and the people, and the extent of his responsiveness to them, cannot be measured by any public opinion polls now in existence. A numerical plurality or even a majority of the people may indicate support for the president. Since the normal impulse is to be loyal to the president because he is president, and to assume that he knows best, anything other than a favorable plurality would indicate deep trouble. However, if the majority of the people are unaware of the existence of a problem or convinced that a solution is impossible, a president's inactivity will not be sufficient to concern them. The existence of a problem requiring presidential action is partly a matter of judgment. President Hoover did not believe that the depression required large-scale presidential or congressional activity, President Roosevelt did. Any leader must be aware of the problems that lie immediately ahead as well as those that have already emerged. The people as a whole may be satisfied with a president who has dealt effectively with current problems while he may be ignoring the somewhat submerged problems of which the electorate is not yet aware. Thus a president who maintains communication only with that segment of the electorate, however large, that supports him and ignores everyone else, must ultimately find himself powerless before the problems that suddenly block his path. It is always the few who first see the issues of tomorrow. It is the problems of today that become the issues of tomorrow; a president unaware of the problems before they become issues cannot hope to begin defining solutions before the problems get out of hand.

Majority rule is a convenience, and the least unacceptable solution to a difficult problem. Majority rule means that the will of the majority must be obeyed and that no minority has a right to impose its will on the majority. It does not mean that the majority is always right, or that the will of the majority today will necessarily be the will of the majority tomorrow. Presidents are elected by a majority, but they are responsible to an electorate beyond only those people who voted for them. No president is elected to do nothing more than represent the popular will; if that were true, the president would have only to take a public opinion poll on every issue and frame his actions accordingly. Clearly, many people have no awareness of pressing problems, no familiarity with proposed solutions, and no criteria with which to choose among them. They designate the president as their surrogate, to translate the current spirit of the people into specific programs, in much the same way that the Supreme Court applies the spirit of the Constitution to cases pending before it. The spirit of the people is not a matter of majorities, but rather the sum of many interests, minorities, and beliefs. It is this spirit that the president supposedly represents and that he will guide toward an understanding of the nation's needs and the best possible way to handle them. This is not to deny the function of pressure groups and the role of intragovernmental politics in the creation of a presidential program, obviously, these are of immense importance. Of equal importance to the demands of powerful interest groups, senior senators, patronage and party leadership, etc., is that which democratic government is supposed to be all about: the will of the people as the expression of what is best for the people. The interest groups are part of "the people"; so are the senators and the party officials and all the rest; but so are those who do not make government part of their everyday concerns, and those who are concerned with government, but are not in power at the moment. Minority interests play a large part in the governing of America; a president who ignores them will discover that he is not leading the country.

"Social justice" has meant bringing disadvantaged groups into the mainstream of American political and economic life. While this goal is yet to be realized, the definition may have to be broadened. Americans are becoming increasingly concerned with the quality of life: with over-crowding, inadequate mass transportation, a poor educational system, pollution, etc. Perhaps one might say that Americans are finally turning from an obsession with *more* to an awareness of *better*. Social justice has to do with the quality of life that is available to all; or, with the justice that society does to each individual's potential. A society that pollutes the air enough to threaten the health of 40 or 50 percent of the population is as unjust as the society that allows 20 percent of its children to remain too poor and too hungry and too sick to be able to learn. The quality of life for most people in the United States is not high compared to what it could be. Presumably, the politics of the near future will be concerned with both consolidating and further advancing the gains of the poor and other minorities and with improving the quality of life for everyone. This implies alterations of the status quo. A president who does not accept responsibility for proposing these alterations will be a president who is largely without issues to fight for and without the need to exercise much power. He will not need close ties with the electorate, for his information requirements will be minimal. It is doubtful whether the country would be able to continue operating if it elected many such presidents.

Conclusion

Thomas E. Cronin has suggested that it is time we divest ourselves of the textbook view of the President as Superman, for in truth, the presidency is simply one part, albeit a prominent one, of the complicated American political system.[1] The fact that no president since World War II has left the White House having accomplished all he set out to do is sufficient testimony to the limitations on any president. Given democratic theory, it is certainly desirable that there be checks on the president (although it is not certain that the current checks are entirely appropriate). A president who took office insistent upon true economic, social, and political justice for all; with a strong program to combat pollution of land, air, and water; committed to major improvements in public transportation; determined to abolish poverty at home and avoid chauvinistic adventures abroad; eager to open the political process to all citizens;—a president who was the embodiment of all current liberal ideals—might well appear to president-watchers as a president who deserved whatever political strength he could amass. It is possible, however, that the president of the United States will at any given moment be a man disinterested in justice, poverty, pollution, the cities, etc. It was pointed out earlier in this essay that to some extent presidential power is cumulative; that is, as presidents involve themselves in aspects of the political process, it becomes traditional for presidents to do so. Thus a tremendously powerful presidency is quite capable of remaining a powerful presidency even if the current president has all the "wrong" ideas.

What is suggested here is that it is far more desirable to have a president limited in his capacity to achieve acceptable goals, than it is to have an unlimited president who could easily achieve unacceptable goals. It is extraordinarily frustrating to see needed programs emasculated by a recalcitrant Congress and unenforced by an uncooperative bureaucracy, especially in a nation that seems to have so much wrong with it, yet it must be recognized that putting vast quantities of power in the hands of one man is extremely dangerous.

It is dangerous not only because the man who acquires the power may use it to further ideas with which one does not agree. It is dangerous because a president is optimally a leader. A tyrant may simply do what he believes is best; a leader persuades his followers that his actions are the best ones. A president unencumbered by congressional and bureaucratic opposition might very well create a legislative program that would, in a platonic sense, be good and wise and just; but by definition, it would also not be democratic. Unless most of the people are unopposed, if not actively in favor of the presidential program, it has no place in a democratic society.

This does not mean that the president must not prod the Congress, the bureaucracy, and the people. Of course he must; he has innumerable possibilities for persuasion and he would be ignoring his responsibilities if he did not use them. But if all his persuasive techniques and devices fail to convince the electorate of the virtue of his program, then that program has no right to exist, that is what democracy means. There is nothing magic about democracy; it does not ensure the triumph of virtue or truth. It is, as Winston Churchill has reputedly suggested, the worst governmental system ever invented except for all the others.

The argument that one can make about the American political system as it currently exists is that its democratic elements are insufficiently democratic. The Congress, for example, would be a far more democratic institution if the seniority system were abolished and small numbers of elderly committee chairmen were no longer able to personally veto proposed legislation. Clearly, the power over domestic policy that the seniority system affords the Congress is extreme. It is not the power to balance the president; all too often, it is the power to ignore him. On the other hand, the power of the president over foreign affairs is not merely the power to balance the Congress; as we have seen, it can become almost a monopoly. The third element in the political system which is less democratic than it ought to be is the bureaucracy, over which the president has insufficient control. Even here, however, total evil is not to be found. If one considers that the only bureaucracy over which the president can be said to have almost total control is the military, and if one considers America's recent history of undeclared wars, it becomes apparent that the president ought not to have complete control of the bureaucracy but that a balance ought to be struck between presidential and congressional control. A possible answer to the problem may lie in President Nixon's recent reorganization of the Bureau of the Budget and his creation of the office of director of Management and Budget.

The president is not superman, nor ought he to be. Nevertheless, it is impossible for the American political system to function properly unless he is prepared to play a positive, dynamic, primary role within it. He is the only nationally elected official; he is chief of state and the symbol of the nation; and whether or not he is a Superman, it is from his office that the people expect solutions to the nation's most pressing problems. He creates a climate of opinion in the country, both by action and inaction; indeed, a president who chooses to do little or nothing creates a climate of opinion by his very inactivity. It is he who sets broad directions for the country by his emphasis of certain problems to the exclusion of others, and necessarily, his decision to emphasize some will mean his down-grading of others. It is he who, because of the wide publicity his acts receive, can make the electorate aware of new problems and it is he who can elicit its support for certain solutions. The White House does not have to be the originator of ideas—the case can probably be made for crediting anyone but public officials with the creation of most important ideas—but it is the chief and most efficient publicizer and cheerleader in American life.

We have already examined presidential power over the budget and the extent to which that power makes his responsible for the direction in which the country is moving. Budgetary power does not mean that the president bears sole responsibility for the country's direction; it does mean that to the extent that any one individual can be credited with an impact on the country's mood, it is his power which is potentially the greatest. Obviously, he is the servant as well as the master, but the gains in presidential popularity which follows almost any strong presidential action indicates that the country is quite willing to be led. One has only to compare the political climate in 1962 or 1965 with that in 1970 to see this.

The president, then, is not and should not be a superman, although much of the country will continue to think of him in that guise. He is a political leader who has far too much unbalanced power over foreign affairs and not nearly enough positive power over domestic policy. He is the one political figure who is constantly in the public eye and who has tremendous power over the climate of opinion in the nation. He runs the constant risk of allowing himself to be cut off from his constituency and of secluding himself so thoroughly in his palatial domain that he becomes unaware of much that is happening in the country. He is in a position that requires continuous activity on his part and yet the fact of continuous activity is no guarantee that his actions will be wise. He has a job whose demands probably cannot be adequately met and yet he is in danger of being surrounded by sycophants whose usefulness will be minimal. It is quite possible that it makes more sense to have a prime minister as a nation's chief executive officer than to have a president who is at the same time chief of state, and yet, the tradition of the presidency is so firmly ensconced in the American political system that it is most unlikely that it will ever be seriously altered. One can only hope that future presidents and Congresses will recognize that his job, and theirs, is impossible without a return to the kind of balance of power which is the hallmark of the democratic state.

Notes

CHAPTER 1

1. Clinton Rossiter, *The American Presidency* (New York: Signet Books, 1956), especially chs. 1 and 4.

2. Richard E. Neustadt, *Presidential Power: The Politics of Leadership* (New York: John Wiley & Sons, 1962).

3. Neustadt, *Presidential Power*, p. 179. *See also* ch. 1.

4. Neustadt, *Presidential Power*, p. 179.

5. Ibid.

6. James Madison, *Debates in the Federal Convention of 1787*, Gaillard Hunt and James B. Scott, eds. (New York: Oxford University Press, 1920), pp. 418-19.

7. Max Farrand, *The Records of the Federal Convention of 1787*, Vol. 2 (New Haven: Yale University Press, 1911), pp. 313, 318-19.

8. Alexander Hamilton in *The Federalist Papers*, number 69.

9. Farrand, *Records of the Federal Convention*, pp. 313, 318-19.

10. Merlo Pusey, *The Way We Go to War* (Boston: Houghton Mifflin Co., 1969), p. 62.

11. Thomas Jefferson in James D. Richardson, ed., *A Compilation of the Messages and Papers of the Presidents, 1789-1897*, vol. 1, 327 (Washington: Government Printing Office, 1896-1899).

12. Richardson, *Messages and Papers of the President*, pp. 389-90.

13. Eugene I. McCormac, *James K. Polk: A Political Biography* (New York: Russell & Russell Publishers, 1965), p. 530.

14. Edward M. Corwin, *The President: Office and Powers*, rev. ed. (New York: N.Y.U. Press, 1957), pp. 229-32. *See also* J. G. Randall, *Constitutional Problems Under Lincoln*, rev. ed. (Urbana, Ill.: University of Illinois Press, 1951), especially chs. 2, 3, 6, 11, and 16.

15. In 1967, Under-Secretary of State Nicholas deB. Katzenbach stated that the resolution when coupled with the SEATO Treaty constituted "the statutory equivalent to a declaration of war." In answering criticism of the war, President Johnson was known to point to a copy of the resolution, which he carried in his pocket, as authorization. *New York Times*, 25 June 1970, p. 3, c. 6.

16. *New York Times*, 2 September 1970, p. 10, c. 2.

17. *New York Times,* 2 September 1970, p. 1, c. 7; p. 2, c. 4.

18. *New York Times,* 9 October 1970, p. 7, c. 1.

19. The one-fifth figure is Robert B. Semple's. *See* the *New York Times,* 13 September 1970, Sect. IV, p. 3, cs. 1-2.

CHAPTER 2

1. *See,* for example, the survey of more than 5,000 students from 39 colleges undertaken by Swarthmore College psychologists Kenneth and Mary Gergen before the Cambodian invasion. They found that almost half the students claimed to have demonstrated against the war. *New York Times,* 21 June 1970, Sect. I, p. 5, c. 1.

2. The growing paucity of Johnson's support on Vietnam is indicated by the Gallup Poll, which asked its selected sample of adults whether they thought the United States had made a mistake in sending troops to Vietnam. In August 1965, 24 percent said *yes* ; March 1966, 25 percent; November 1966, 31 percent; February 1967, 32 percent; December 1967, 45 percent; August 1968, 53 percent. In May 1970, when the war had become "Nixon's war," 56 percent answered *yes* and only 8 percent had no opinion (as opposed to 15 percent with no opinion in August 1965). *New York Times,* 28 June 1970, Sect. I, p. 4, cs. 1-3.

3. *See,* e.g., Philip E. Converse and Howard Schuman, "Silent Majorities and the Vietnam War," *Scientific American,* June 1970, pp. 17-25. The conclusion of the authors, based on a study done at the Survey Research Center of the University of Michigan, was that, on the Vietnam issue, presidential popularity rose whenever the president took the initiative — no matter whether his action escalated or deescalated the war. Not too long before President Nixon sent troops into Cambodia, the Gallup Poll found that only 28 percent of Americans would approve such action. The Harris Poll found only 7 percent. Once the action was taken, however, both polls found that a majority were in favor of it. Cited by Clayton Fritchey in the *New York Post,* 22 June 1970, p. 41. According to the Gallup Poll, on June 19-21, 1970, 55 percent of the electorate thought the president was doing a good job. The sample taken July 10-12, after the Cambodia pull-out, showed his popularity at 61 percent. A period of inactivity followed, and by July 31-August 2 the figure had slipped back to 55 percent. *New York Times,* 20 August 1970, p. 20, c. 3.

4. For a fuller discussion of the Dominican Republic crisis, *see* Tad Szulc, *Dominican Diary* (New York: Delacorte Press, 1965). *See also* Rowland Evans and Robert Novack, *Lyndon B. Johnson: The Exercise of Power* (New York: The New American Library, 1966), ch. 23.

5. Arthur M. Schlesinger, Jr., *A Thousand Days: John F. Kennedy in the White House* (Boston: Houghton Mifflin Co., 1965).

6. Schlesinger *A Thousand Days,* p. 812. Kennedy added, however, "When you can talk to them individually, they are reasonable." Ibid. Individual conferences might therefore be helpful, but it is doubtful that any president would have the time for many of them.

7. Senator Jacob Javits, along with Senators Pell, Spong, and Mathias, has recently introduced a bill permitting the president to meet military emergencies with the use of force. An emergency would be an attack on the United States or on American troops abroad, the necessity to protect the lives and property of Americans abroad, or the need to comply with a treaty obligation. Such hostilities could not be continued for more than 30 days, however, with Congressional authorization. The bill, previously introduced in 1970, has some hope of Senate passage in the light of attempts by conservative members (such as Senator Stennis, for example) to find a way of limiting the Presidential war power without crippling it. S. 731 (1971) Congressional Record, 92nd Congress, 1st session. Feb. 10, 1971.

CHAPTER 3

1. For a more detailed account of public actions taken by Department personnel, *see* Philippa Strum, "Forward Together: The Nixon Administration on Integration," *Afro-American Studies* 2 (Summer 1970): 161; and Peter Gall, "The Culture of Bureaucracy: Mores of Protest," *Washington Monthly* 4 (June 1970): 75.

2. Senator William O. Proxmire, *Report from Wasteland: America's Military-Industrial Complex* (New York: Frederick A. Praeger, 1970), p. 63.

3. Proxmire, *Report from Wasteland,* p. 62.

4. Ibid., p. 63.

5. Ibid.

6. *New York Times,* 7 May 1968, p. 1, c. 7.

7. *New York Times,* 1 December 1968, p. 22, c. 4.

8. In July 1970, Secretary of Defense Melvin Laird announced that entire defense contracts would no longer be handed out only when development of a new weapon reached the point where the final product seemed workable. That was the system utilized during the preceding two decades. Developments during the postcontract period often led to expensive changes in design and led to high cost overruns. Twelve major weapons systems included in a Harvard Business School study, for example, had an average overrun of 20 percent of the estimated cost. The new system will involve developing and fully testing a weapon before it is put into production. Unfortunately, this may not result in significant savings, since it implies that contracts will be handed out on a piecemeal basis that will prevent public and Congress from knowing the full price for the entire purchase for some time. *See* the article by Neil Sheehan in the *New York Times,* 1 August 1970, p. 7, cs. 1-4, from which these statistics were taken. *See also* the criticism of the proposed system by A. Ernest Fitzgerald, former deputy for Management and Systems, Department of the Air Force. "Gilbert Fitzhugh's Golden Fleece," *Washington Monthly,* November 1970, p. 44.

9. Proxmire, *Report from Wasteland,* pp. 153-61.

10. *New York Times,* 13 August 1970, p. 13, cs. 1 and 2.

11. Schlesinger, *A Thousand Days,* p. 709.

12. It is possible but by no means certain that Congress is interested in reasserting its authority. The various measures proposed in the Senate to curb presidential involvement of American forces abroad are one indication of such interst. Others include the August 1971 attempt by the Senate Foreign Relations Committee to cut off funds for the foreign aid program unless the Pentagon supplied the committee with its five-year military assistance plan, which it had previously refused to allow the committee to see; the Senate-approved Mansfield amendment to the draft bill, mandating a date for troop withdrawal from Vietnam; and the legislation proposed by Senators Case and Symington to prevent the president's use of undisclosed CIA funds to fight the secret war in Laos. At the same time, however, recent articles indicate that dovish senators have taken few concrete steps to curtail American participation in the Indochina War and that only a handful of legislators have bothered to look at the complete set of Pentagon Papers deposited with Congress. See John Rothchild, "Cooling Down the War: The Senates Lame Doves," *Washington Monthly* 3. (August 1971): 6; and Walter Pincus, "After the Pentagon Papers—The Same Old Story," *New York,* 16 August 1971, p. 46.

CHAPTER 4

1. Roger Hilsman, *To Move a Nation* (New York: Doubleday & Co., 1967), pp. 202-3.

2. Ibid., pp. 34-35.

3. Ibid., pp. 75-76.

4. Ibid., p. 34.

5. Ibid., p. 116.

6. Robert Sherrill: "Why Can't We Just Give Them Food?" in *New York Times Magazine,* 22 March 1970, p. 28.

7. *New York Times* 31 March 1970, p. 17, cs. 2-6.

8. Sherrill, "Why Can't We Just Give Them Food?" p. 98.

9. Ibid.

10. Quoted in Sherrill, "Why Can't We Just Give Them Food?"

11. Ibid., p. 93.

12. The idea of a triumverate or a three-way relationship has been expressed as "subgovernments" by Douglass Cater in *Power in Washington* (New York: Random House, 1964), as "policy whirlpools" by Ernest S. Griffith in *Congress, Its Contemporary Role* (New York: New York University Press, 1961), and as "cozy little triangles" by Dorothy Buckton James in *The Contemporary Presidency* (New York: Pegasus Publishers, 1969).

CHAPTER 5

1. The following account of the 1968 meeting of the "Senior Advisory Group on Vietnam" and its impact on the president draws primarily on three sources: the articles in the *New York Times* of March 6 and 7, 1969, reprinted in the Appendix; Townsend Hoopes, *The Limits of Intervention* (New York: David McKay Co., 1969), pp.207, 214-18; and Theodore H. White, *The Making of the President 1968* (New York: Atheneum Publishers, 1969), pp. 129-30.

2. Hoopes, *The Limits of Intervention,* p. 217.

3. White, *The Making of the President,* p. 130.

4. Ibid.

5. Hoopes, *The Limits of Intervention,* p. 61. *See also* pp. 59, 60, and 116.

6. White, *The Making of the President,* p. 126.

7. George Christian, *The President Steps Down* (New York: Macmillan Co., 1970), p. 115.

8. Louis Heren. *No Hail, No Farewell* (New York: Harper & Row Publishers), p. 185.

9. This view has been challenged by Professor John P. Roche, who was a member of the White House staff during the Johnson Administration ("The Jigsaw Puzzle of History" in *New York Times Magazine,* 24 January 1971, p. 14). Roche makes the very useful point that "insider" accounts of the presidency necessarily constitute no more than pieces of a puzzle that is never seen in its entirety by any one person. He further argues that Johnson was accessible to such advisers as Roche, who consistently opposed the bombing of North Vietnam, and that Secretary of State Dean Rusk had been sympathetic to a partial bombing halt as early as November 1967. Roche does not deal with two important considerations; i.e., the lack of anyone who opposed the entire war effort, rather than particular strategies, within or with access to the White House circle; and the reliance on information from top Pentagon officials who had helped design the Vietnam strategy and who therefore can be presumed to have had a stake in defending it.

10. Robert B. Semple, Jr., *New York Times Magazine,* 19 March 1969, p. 122.

11. *New York Times,* 26 November 1970, p. 23, c. 2.

12. Semple in *New York Times,* 18 September, p. 16, c. 4.

13. Ibid.

14. *New York Times,* 26 November 1970, p. 23, c. 1.

15. *New York Times,* 15 December 1970, p. 22, c. 6. The article, written by Robert B. Semple, Jr., implies that the move represented a device aimed at the 1972 campaign rather than a change in Nixon's thinking.

16. Robert F. Kennedy, *Thirteen Days* (New York: W. W. Norton & Co. 1968), p. 112.

17. Ibid.

18. Heren, *No Hail, No Farewell,* p. 17.

19. Ibid.

20. Theodore C. Sorensen, *Kennedy* (New York: Harper & Row, Publishers, 1965), pp. 258, 260.

21. Sorensen, *Kennedy,* p. 372.

22. This account is based on the invaluable article by Robert B. Semple, Jr., in the *New York Times,* 19 March 1969, p. 72, cs. 1-6.

23. Ibid.

24. This information is included in a column about presidential isolation that should be read by anyone interested in the subject. It appeared on the editorial page of the *New York Times,* 4 November 1969.

25. Richard F. Fenno, Jr. *The President's Cabinet* (New York: Random House, Inc. 1959), p. 69.

26. This refers to Richard Fenno.

27. President Nixon's proposed reorganization of the cabinet, while unlikely to be implemented soon, would in any event do no more than alter the status of the people with whom the president ought to consult. The lesser number of secretaries would still constitute a broad spectrum of opinion, but the officials most directly responsive to and representative of interest groups would undoubtedly be the new section and bureau chiefs.

28. Mary McGrory in the *New York Post,* 11 January 1971, p. 31.

29. Ibid.

30. See the article in the *New York Times* on the relationship between President Nixon and the Congress. July 12, 1970, Sect. IV, p. 3, cs. 3-5.

31. *New York Times,* 16 January 1971, p. 15, c. 4. In August 1971, when President Nixon became angry at the lack of congressional action on his priority domestic legislation, MacGregor stopped wearing his button. *New York Times,* 8 August 1971, Sect. IV, p. 2, c. 7.

32. *New York Times,* 24 July 1970, p. 4, c. 5.

33. Tom Wicker in the *New York Times,* 25 November 1969.

34. *New York Times,* 9 August 1970, Sect. IV, p. 4, c. 1.

35. *New York Times,* 24 July 1970, p. 4, c. 3.

36. Stuart Symington, "Congress's Right to Know," *New York Times Magazine,* 9 August 1970, p. 63.

37. Ibid., p. 62.

38. Ibid.

39. Ibid.

40. *New York Times,* 28 July 1970, p. 4, c. 4.

41. *New York Times,* 21 August 1970, p. 1, c. 5; p. 7. c. 1.

42. Ibid., p. 7, c. 1.

43. Symington, "Congress's Right to Know," p. 65. See also the report submitted by Senator Symington's subcommittee after its two-year study. *Congressional Record,* 91st Congress, 2nd Session, December 9, 1970.

44. *New York Times,* 30 August 1970, Sect. IV, p. 1, c. 1.

45. Ibid. See also *New York Times,* 16 August 1970, Sect. IV, p. 6, cs. 1-2.

46. Walter Goldstein, "Skepticism on Capitol Hill; The Congress Revives Its Role as a Critic of National Security Policy," *Virginia Quarterly Review,* Summer 1970, p. 390.

47. Heren, *No Hail, No Farewell,* p. 74.

CHAPTER 6

1. Schlesinger, *A Thousand Days,* p. 717.

2. Sorensen, *Kennedy* p. 316. See also Schlesinger, *A Thousand Days,* pp. 675, 676.

3. Sorensen, p. 378.

4. Christian, *The President Steps Down,* p. 6.

5. For a history of the modern presidential press conference, *see* Douglass Cater, "The President and the Press," *Annals of the American Academy of Political and Social Science* September 1956, pp. 55-65.

6. Louis Koenig, *The Chief Executive,* rev. ed. (New York: Harcourt Brace Jovanovich, 1968), p. 196. *See also* Arthur M. Schlesinger, Jr., *The Coming of the New Deal* (Boston: Houghton Mifflin Co., 1959), p. 561.

7. Schlesinger, *The Coming of the New Deal,* p. 561.

8. Ibid.

9. Schlesinger, *A Thousand Days,* p. 716.

10. Theodore H. White, *The Making of the President 1960* (New York: Atheneum Publishers, 1961).

11. Much of the test and the circumstances surrounding Nixon's statement to the press are to be found in Jules Witcover, *The Resurrection of Richard Nixon* (New York: G. P. Putnam's Sons, 1970), pp. 13-22.

12. *New York Times,* 31 July 1970, p. 10, c. 1.

13. Ibid., c. 7.

14. Ibid.

15. Sorensen, *Kennedy,* pp. 325-26.

16. Worth Bingham and Ward S. Just, "The President and the Press," *Reporter,* 12 April 1962, p. 21.

17. It may also be an indication of his relationship with the bureaucracy. Max Frankel reports that one of President Kennedy's reasons for holding regular news conferences was that the bureaucracy had to brief him beforehand and thus reveal the potentially embarrassing matters that the bureaucrats might have preferred to hide. *New York Times,* 10 December 1970, p. 22, c. 4.

18. *New York Times,* 3 August 1970, p. 16, cs. 7-8.

19. Bingham and Just, "The President and the Press," p. 19.

20. For an account of his attempt and failure, *see* Rowland Evans and Robert Novak, *Lyndon B. Johnson: The Exercise of Power* (New York: New American Library, 1966), pp. 411-12.

21. *New York Times,* 3 August 1970, p. 16, c. 3. *See also* Christian, *The President Steps Down,* pp. 202-3.

22. The attitude was noticed by James Reston, who is quoted by Bingham and Just, *The President Steps Down,* p. 21.

23. Robert B. Semple, Jr. in the *New York Times,* 30 August, Sect. IV, p. 4, c. 1.

24. *New York Times,* August 24, 1970, p. 18, c. 1.

25. Ibid.

26. *See* TRB, "Who's Top Briefer?" in *New Republic,* 12 September 1970, p. 6. *See also New York Times,* 30 August 1970, Sect. IV, p. 4., c. 1.

27. Hedrick Smith, "When the President Meets the Press," in *Atlantic,* August 1970, p. 67.

28. John Osborne, *The Nixon Watch* (New York: Liveright Publishing Corp., 1970), p. 16.

29. Osborne, *The Nixon Watch,* p. 85.

30. Ibid., p. 88.

31. Robert B. Semple, Jr., "Nixon's Presidency Is a Very Private Affair," *New York Times Magazine,* 2 November 1969, p. 120.

32. *New York Times,* 24 August 1970, p. 18, c. 1.

33. Sorensen, *Kennedy* pp. 332-33.

34. Ibid., p. 332.

35. *New York Times,* 24 May 1970, Scct. IV, p. 2, c. 5.

36. Ibid., c. 7.

37. Ibid., c. 5.

38. *New York Times,* 22 June 1970, p. 33, cs. 1-2.

39. *New York Times,* 24 May Sect. IV, p. 2, c. 5.

40. Ibid.

41. Clayton Fritchey in the *New York Post,* 22 June 1970, p. 41.

42. Semple, "Nixon's Presidency," p. 124.

43. George E. Reedy, *The Twilight of the Presidency* (New York: World Publishing Co. 1970).

44. Hugh Sidey, *John F. Kennedy, President* (New York: Atheneum Publishers), pp. 208-9.

45. Heren, *No Hail, No Farewell*, p. 29.

46. Jack Anderson in the *New York Post*, 7 July 1970, p. 44.

47. *New York Post*, 18 August 1970, p. 53, c. 5.

48. *New York Times*, 19 August 1970, p. 1, c. 5; p. 19, c. 1.

49. Robert B. Semple, Jr., in the *New York Times*, 3 October 1970, p. 3, cs. 1-3.

50. John Osborne in *New Republic*, 17 October 1970, p. 8.

51. *New York Times*, 12 January 1970, p. 32, c. 2.

52. Quoted in *New York Times*, 24 July 1970, p. 13, c. 5.

53. John Osborne quotes one of President Nixon's assistants as describing the president as the kind of person who believes " 'If everyone will just keep quiet and leave me alone, I'll get it done and everything will be all right.' " Osborne, *The Nixon Watch*, p. 85.

CHAPTER 7

1. *See*, e.g., Louis W. Koenig, *The Chief Executive*, rev. ed. (New York: Harcourt Brace Jovanovich, 1968), pp. 10-12; Grant McConnell, *The Modern Presidency* (New York: St. Martin's Press, 1967), ch. I. These choices are arbitrary; the dichotomy runs through most works on the presidency written since the New Deal.

2. Quoted in Koenig, *The Chief Executive*, p. 302.

3. Quoted in James MacGregor Burns, "The One Test for the Presidency," *New York Times Magazine*, 1 May 1960, p. 102.

4. Koenig, *The Chief Executive*, p. 192.

5. Heren, *No Hail, No Farewelll*, p. 180.

6. Christian, *The President Steps Down*, p. 258.

7. Quoted in Robert Wool, "Still the Man Who Loves to Talk, to Teach, to Preach," in *New York Times Magazine*, 11 October 1970, p. 26.

CONCLUSION

1. Thomas E. Cronin, "Superman, Our Textbook President," *Washington Monthly*, October 1970, p. 47.

Appendix I

Presidential Decision-making: President Johnson
For a Bombing Halt and Against Seeking Reelection

THE VIETNAM POLICY REVERSAL OF 1968: PART I

On the cold and cheerless early morning of February 28, 1968, the Chairman of the Joint Chiefs of Staff, Gen. Earle G. Wheeler, landed at Andrews Air Force Base after an urgent mission to Saigon. Pausing only to change into a fresh uniform, he hurried through the rain to the White House to deliver a report and make a request.

The report was designed to encourage an anxious President and his beleaguered advisers, but it served only to shock them into extended debate.

The request—for more troops—was designed to bring military victory at last in the eight-year American military effort, but it led instead to a fateful series of decisions that stand in retrospect as one of the most remarkable turnabouts in United States foreign policy.

The month of March, 1968, became a watershed for a nation and a Government in turmoil. The Johnson Administration, by pulling back from the brink of deeper commitments and moving toward disengagement, set a course that affects the daily decisions of the Nixon Administration.

Many of the ingredients of decision then—troop strength and what to do about bombing North Vietnam—are still live issues, and many of the principal actors involved a year ago are participants in yet another crucial policy debate on Vietnam.

This Appendix reprints two articles originally published in *The New York Times* of March 6, and 7, 1969. They were written by Hendrick Smith in collaboration with William Beecher, and incorporate reports by Peter Grose, John W. Finney, E. W. Kenworthy, Roy Reed, Benjamin Welles, Edwin L. Dale Jr. and Max Frankel. ©1969 by The New York Times Company. Reprinted by permission.

On that day at the end of February, President Johnson and his closest aides assembled for breakfast around the Chippendale table in the elegant family dining room on the second floor of the Executive Mansion. Before rising from the table, they had set in motion the most intensive policy review of the Johnson Presidency—and one of the most agonizing of any Presidency.

The wrenching debate began almost by accident and then gained a momentum all its own. One dramatic record of its progress appeared in the 12 versions of a Presidential speech that evolved during the month—the last draft pointing in the opposite direction from the first.

The entire episode also provided a remarkable demonstration of how foreign policy is battled out, inch by inch, by negotiation rather than decision. The turnabout emerged through sharp confrontations and subtle, even conspiratorial, maneuvering—with compromises struck for bureaucratic purposes and with opponents in agreement for contrary reasons.

At the time of that breakfast meeting, President Johnson had been thinking for about two months about not seeking re-election. His principal advisers had little inkling of his thoughts, and the President himself had no expectation that the tensions in the Government would shatter the concensus of his inner circle.

Clark M. Clifford, appointed but not yet sworn in as Secretary of Defense, was to play the pivotal role in the Vietnam reassessment, but it was not a one man show.

CLIFFORD UNDER PRESSURE

Mr. Clifford had to be persuaded. He immediately came under pressure from a faction of civilian dissenters at the Pentagon who believed the war was deadlocked, questioned American objectives and felt that time to salvage American policy was fast running out.

When the debate was over, the President had set the Government on the path toward peace negotiations and disengagement from the war. He had imposed a limit on the military commitment to South Vietnam, ordered a reduction in the bombing of North Vietnam, and offered to negotiate with the Hanoi regime. And he had coupled the offer with the announcement of his withdrawal from the 1968 political campaign.

The replacement of the quest for military victory with the search for compromise might have been reversed by North Vietnam if it had not—to almost everyone's surprise—responded favorably to Mr. Johnson's offer. Furthermore, the hawkish faction in the White House inner circle sought to resist the new trend until the Johnson Administration left office in January.

The catalytic event in the policy reappraisal—and the centerpiece of General Wheeler's vivid report—was the enemy's Lunar New Year offensive, which began January 30, 1968, and swelled into coordinated assaults on 36 South Vietnamese cities and included, in Saigon, a bold penetration of the United States Embassy compound.

CONFIDENCE IS SHATTERED

Confident and secure one day, Gen. William C. Westmoreland, then the American commander in Saigon, found himself on the next dealing with a vast battle the length of South Vietnam.

The psychological impact on Washington had outrun the event: The capital was stunned. But General Wheeler, with murals of the American Revolution behind him, offered a more reassuring picture to the White House breakfast on February 28.

The Tet attacks had not caused a military defeat, he said. The enemy had been thrown back with heavy losses and had failed to spark a popular uprising against the South Vietnamese regime. Not only had the Government in Saigon and its army survived the hurricane, he continued, but the offensive has "scared the living daylights," out of non-Communists, and they were beginning to cooperate.

On the other hand, the general said that more—many more—American troops were needed because the allied forces were off balance and vulnerable to another offensive.

General Westmoreland felt, General Wheeler reported, that massive reinforcements would guard against a quick repetition of the Tet offensive and would allow the allies to regain the initiative, to exploit the enemy's losses and to "speed the course of the war to our objectives."

General Wheeler gave the Westmoreland request his personal endorsement. It added up to 206,000 more men.

A BIG "SHOPPING LIST"

General Westmoreland, who did not actually use the figure, regarded the proposal as a planning paper. But President Johnson and other officials, knowing that, as a matter of administrative technique, no request became formal until the President had decided how many troops would be sent, treated the Westmoreland paper as a request. Even without a precise total they sensed how much was being sought. The "shopping list" outlined by General Wheeler called for three more combat divisions, with sizable air, naval and land support.

Once the plan was fed through the Pentagon computers the precise number emerged. It became so secret that to this day some officials will not utter it—a reminder of the President's wrath when it did leak to the press during the March debate.

The sheer size of the request—a 40 percent increase in the 535,000-man force committed to Vietnam—stunned Mr. Johnson and the civilians around him, though the initial impulse was to see how the commander's needs might be filled.

"It was a hell of a serious breakfast," one participant recalled. "It was rough as a cob!"

Some of the participants believed that a substantial troop increase could well revive arguments for widening the war—for giving General Westmoreland permission to go after enemy sanctuaries on the ground in Cambodia and Laos, and perhaps even in North Vietnam.

The President was wary about a massive new commitment. Had he not gone to extraordinary lengths to send half a million men to Vietnam without calling up reserves or imposing economic controls? Every year the generals had come to him—sometimes more than once a year—with the plea for "a little bit more to get the job done." Now, with the nation sharply divided over the war, they were asking for mobilization.

They had confronted Mr. Johnson with a dilemma. The gist of the Wheeler-Westmoreland report, in the words of one breakfast guest was blunt: "We've got to have a big infusion of troops or we can't achieve our objectives."

No one at the breakfast table that day advocated lowering objectives. It was a time, however, when many pressures for a change of course were converging on the White House.

SPREADING DOUBTS ABOUT WAR

The Tet offensive had punctured the heady optimism over the military progress reported to Congress by General Westmoreland and by Ellsworth Bunker, the Ambassador to South Vietnam, in November, 1967. Not only had the pool of disenchantment spread by late February to fence-sitters in Congress, to newspaper offices and to business organizations. It had also reached the upper echelons of the Government.

If tolerance of the war had worn thin, so had the nation's military resources—so thin, indeed, that there was almost nothing more to send to Vietnam without either mobilizing, enlarging draft calls, lengthening the 12-month combat tour or sending Vietnam veterans back for second tours of duty—all extremely unappealing.

Congress was in such ferment that the process of legislation was partly paralyzed. The dollar was being battered by the gold crisis in Europe and inflation at home.

More fundamentally, the nation was seriously divided. The fabric of public civility had begun to unravel as opinion on the war polarized.

President Johnson chose his long-time friend, Clark Clifford, to head a task force to advise him on the troop request. It quickly became a forum for debating the entire rationale for the war.

At 10:30 A.M. on Friday, March 1, in the East room of the White House, Mr. Clifford took the oath of office as the successor to Robert S. McNamara. Three hours later he gathered the task force around the oval oak table in the private Pentagon dining room of the Secretary of Defense.

Secretary of State Dean Rusk, for the first time in his seven years in office, went to the Defense Department for a formal meeting.

The others present were all, like Mr. Rusk, veterans of arguments on Vietnam policy—Walt W. Rostow, the President's assistant for national security affairs; Richard Helms, Director of Central Intelligence; General Wheeler, General

Maxwell D. Taylor, former Chairman of the Joint Chiefs of Staff, former Ambassador to Saigon and a Presidential adviser on Vietnam; Paul H. Nitze, Deputy Secretary of Defense; Under Secretary of State Nicholas deB. Katzenbach; Paul C. Warnke, Assistant Secretary of Defense for International Security Affairs; Phil G. Goulding, Assistant Secretary of Defense for Public Affairs; William P. Bundy, Assistant Secretary of State for East Asian Affairs; and, for financial advice, the Secretary of the Treasury, Henry H. Fowler.

None of the civilians present advocated a flat commitment of 206,000 more men, nor did they want to reject the request out of hand. Several insiders later suggested that a smaller request, for 30,000 to 50,000 men, would probably have been granted and the Administration crisis would have been avoided, or at least delayed.

Instead there was an early collision in the task force over war strategy and the possibilities of victory. There were shadings of viewpoint on most questions, but two broad coalitions emerged:

One favored continuation of General Westmoreland's strategy of wearing down the enemy by intense military pounding. The argument's assumption was that the Tet situation was less a setback than an opportunity. By boldly seizing the initiative, according to this view, the allies could decimate and demoralize the enemy and open the way to a favorable settlement.

The other group challenged the very premises of the old strategy. Its members urged a less aggressive ground war, called for new efforts to open negotiations and, implicitly, laid the groundwork for political compromise.

The exponents of continuity were Mr. Rusk and Mr. Rostow and Generals Wheeler and Taylor. Mr. Rusk, by then the stanchest defender of the war in public, patiently bore the heat of criticism. Tall, unbending, composed, he was, in his own words, "the iceman."

ROSTOW FILTERED THE NEWS

Mr. Rostow and General Taylor, who had gone to Vietnam early in 1961 as President Kennedy's personal envoys and who came back advocating intervention, were even more opposed to "letting up the pressure." Mr. Rostow, athletic and ebullient, funneled the news from Saigon to the President.

The advocates of change were Messrs. Nitze, Warnke, and Katzenbach, and later—most powerfully—Mr. Clifford. Mr. Helms, thoughtful and angular, was neutral on policy questions. The weight of his C.I.A. analysis called into question military judgments, past strategy and the quest for victory implicit in so many earlier decisions.

Although Mr. Clifford was never alone, his eventual role was remarkable because it was wholly unexpected.

He came into government with a reputation as a hawk, as a trusted, loyal "back-room" counselor to Mr. Johnson who had steadfastly supported Administration policy. In December, 1965, he had opposed the 36-day bombing pause then advocated by his predecessor. One man acquainted with the circumstances of the Clifford appointment said later:

"I am sure the President felt, 'Here is a good, strong, sturdy supporter of the war, and that's what I need.' McNamara was wobbling—particularly on the bombing issue. I think the President felt Clifford was strong and sturdy."

But Mr. Clifford had begun to have doubts during a trip in August, 1967, to Vietnam and allied countries contributing troops to the war. On his return he confided to the President that he was deeply uneasy at having discovered that the American view of the war was not fully shared by Australia, New Zealand, Thailand and the Philippines.

Disturbed he was, but he remained a supporter of Administration policy. He was encouraged by secret diplomatic efforts in August, 1967, and again in January, 1968, to get negotiations with Hanoi started on the basis of the so-called San Antonio formula.

That proposal, made public by President Johnson in a speech in the Texas city on September 30, 1967, offered to halt the bombing of North Vietnam provided it would lead promptly to productive talks and "assuming" that Hanoi would not take military advantage of the cessation.

At Mr. Clifford's Senate confirmation hearings on January 25, 1968, he had added the important interpretation that this meant that the President would tolerate "normal" levels of infiltration from North to South Vietnam.

The President had not cleared Mr. Clifford's remarks in advance and, as a result, according to one informed source, "all hell broke loose at the White House and the State Department."

Secretary Rush was said to have argued for two days with President Johnson against giving Administration endorsement to the interpretation. He was overruled. On Jan. 29 the State Department said Mr. Clifford's remarks represented United States policy.

He plunged into the minutiae of Vietnam like a lawyer taking a new case. He had private talks with Mr. McNamara, whose own misgivings had sharpened in his final months at the Pentagon.

As a newcomer with limited knowledge, Mr. Clifford had to rely on civilian subordinates more than had his brilliant and experienced predecessor. The large faction of dissenters from Administration policy was quick to seize the opportunity to press its views. The Tet offensive, recalled one dissenter, "gave us something we could hang our arguments on, something to contradict the beguiling upward curve on the progress charts" from Saigon.

"HIDDEN DOVES" DISCOVERED

With the lid off, the new Secretary discovered a nest of "hidden doves" at the Pentagon, including his deputy, Mr. Nitze; Assistant Secretaries Warnke, Alain C. Enthoven, Goulding and Alfred B. Fitt; the Under Secretaries of the Army, Navy and Air Force—David E. McGiffert, Charles F. Baird and Townsend W. Hoopes; a few younger generals and colonels and a score of young civilians brought in by Mr. McNamara, principally Dr. Morton H. Halperin, Dr. Leslie H. Gelb and Richard C. Steadman.

The men who clearly had the greatest impact on the new Secretary's thinking were Messrs. Nitze, Warnke and Goulding—perhaps Mr. Warnke more than the others.

"Warnke was deeply upset about Vietnam and he was persuasive," a colleague said. "His style and Mr. Clifford's meshed." As a measure of their mutual confidence, Mr. Clifford chose Mr. Warnke as a law partner when both left the Government.

When the Clifford task force got under way, a number of officials took the troop request as evidence of panic on General Westmoreland's part. But ranking officers who were in Saigon headquarters during and after the Tet offensive assert that there was no thought of asking for many more troops until shortly before General Wheeler's visit late in February.

"The President asked General Wheeler to go out to Vietnam to find out what General Westmoreland thought he could use," a Pentagon official said. Civilian officials were irritated by this approach. "It was a mistake to ask a damned-fool question like that," a State Department official remarked.

The Joint Chiefs of Staff had their own reasons for favoring a massive increase and a reserve call-up. For months they had been deeply concerned that the strategic reserve had been dangerously depleted and they had been looking for a chance to reconstitute it by persuading the President to mobilize National Guard units.

Another view was held by Ambassador Bunker, who never fully endorsed the troop request and who wanted first priority for re-equipping and expanding the South Vietnamese Army—a suggestion endorsed by Pentagon civilians.

The Wheeler-Westmoreland plan presented to the task force called for 206,000 men by June 30, 1969—roughly 100,000 within a few months and two later increments of about 50,000 men each. The first segment was to come from available active-duty units in the United States; the rest were to come from the reserves.

In the view of the Joint Chiefs, only the full number would assure victory. The implication was that with 206,000 more men, the war would "not be terribly long," as one Pentagon civilian put it—but there was no precise forecast.

At this point Mr. Warnke, in his nasal Massachusetts accent, read a paper that challenged the military thesis head on. Hanoi, he said, would match American reinforcements as it had in the past, and the result would simply be escalation and "a lot more killing" on both sides.

Besides, the task force was told, the financial costs would be immense. The proposed scale of reinforcements would add nearly $10 billion to a war already costing $30 billion a year.

As an alternative, Mr. Warnke urged a turn toward de-escalation—a pullback from General Westmoreland's aggressive search-and-destroy tactics and the abandonment of isolated outposts like the besieged Marine garrison at Khesanh. He said that American forces should be used as a mobile shield in and around population centers and that more should be demanded from the South Vietnamese Army.

The sheer complexity of the troop issue began to raise doubts in Mr. Clifford's mind.

QUESTIONS OTHERS AVOIDED

"Part of it was Clark's intelligent questioning and part of it was his naivete," a colleague recalled. "He asked about things that others more familiar with the details would not have asked.

"He just couldn't get the figures straight on troops. He drove Bus Wheeler mad. He would say, 'Now I understand you wanted 22,000 men for such and such,' and Wheeler would point out this didn't include the support elements, and if you added them, it would be 35,000 in all."

"This happened again and again every time Clark wanted to get the numbers down as low as possible, and it had a psychological impact on him," the source added.

The first weekend in March was consumed by a study of the papers drafted for the task force and by questions. "It was meet all day, sandwiches in for lunch, sandwiches in for dinner," a participant recalled.

Word was passed to President Johnson that the review "wasn't going well" and had hit a "discordant note." But Mr. Clifford's doubts had not hardened into conviction by the time he handed the President his first report on March 5.

A short, unsigned, four-or-five-page memorandum, it recommended giving General Westmoreland 50,000 more troops in the next three months and set out a schedule for readying the rest of the 200,000 men for dispatch over the next 15 months.

FROM DIVERGENT POINTS OF VIEW

Characteristically, the President's advisers disagreed on the recommendation's significance. The Pentagon saw it as a move "to get the pipeline going"- general approval of the troop request; State Department officials viewed it as part of a process of "whittling down" the 206,000 figure.

Although Mr. Clifford had passed along the report, he was uneasy about it. He was worried that if the President approved the first batch of troops, that action would move him irrevocably toward the whole 206,000. But the Secretary did not challenge the report directly; he tried to stall, suggesting that the task force check General Westmoreland's reaction to be sure the "mix" of forces was right.

General Wheeler wanted to move ahead, but others, including Mr. Rusk and Mr. Rostow, were willing to have the issue studied further, so the task force carried on for several more days.

This seemed to suit Mr. Johnson's mood, too. His instinct, a White House aide explained later, was to delay implementing the plan. "He kept putting off making an initial decision," the aide said.

For the President had heard the grumbles in Congress over the danger to the dollar from the gold drain and from the rising costs of the war. Politicians were alarmed by the size of the troop request.

Old trusted friends like Senator Richard B. Russell, the Georgia Democrat who headed the Armed Services Committee, were complaining tartly about General Westmoreland. Influential men like Senator John Stennis, the Mississippi Democrat, were privately warning the President to go slow on mobilizing reserves.

As the task force persisted, Secretary Clifford himself was putting more pointed questions. "What is our military plan for victory?" he asked. "How will we end the war?" He was not satisfied.

Then the bombing compaign came under his scrutiny. Mr. Hoopes wrote him a memorandum urging a halt, arguing that the bombing was not having significant results and that, because of Soviet and Chinese Communist aid, North Vietnam had become "on balance a stronger military power today than before the bombing began."

Mr. Hoopes contended that it was "a military fiction" that American combat casualties would rise if the bombing were halted. American losses, he said, were primarily a result of the aggressive ground strategy in the South.

Under the impact of such arguments, Mr. Clifford's doubts became convictions. He supported the President's previous restrictions on the war—no invasion of North Vietnam, no expansion of the ground war into Laos or Cambodia, no mining of the Haiphong harbor—and he became convinced that within those restrictions there was no military answer. He began the search for a path to disengagement.

The debate, by now in the White House, seesawed through the middle of March. At this time Mr. Clifford began to state his case for a fundamental change in American policy: It was time to emphasize peace, not a larger war.

He now challenged the task-force recommendation for more troops. "This isn't the way to go at all," he told the President. "This is all wrong."

HIS WORDS CARRIED WEIGHT

With the nation bitterly divided over the war and in desperate need at home, he maintained, it would be immoral to consider enormous added investment in Vietnam—a "military sinkhole."

His outspoken challenge was deeply disturbing to President Johnson, who always preferred a consensus among his close advisers. Although he never turned his celebrated temper on Mr. Clifford, the argument chilled their personal relations and left the Defense Secretary, a friend for 30 years, feeling oddly frozen out of the White House at times.

Secretary Rusk apparently did not disagree with Mr. Clifford so sharply on troop numbers, but he was opposed to the long-run implications of Mr. Clifford's arguments—that in the end, the United States would have to settle for less. Mr. Rostow felt that the new Defense Secretary had fallen under the influence of "the professional pessimists" in the Defense Department.

At the Pentagon, morale was rising among civilian advocates of a new policy. "We used to ask," a former Pentagon civilian said of the Secretary, "is he one of us? Well, there was 'one of us' at the White House." He was Harry McPherson, the President's speech drafter, who, unknown to the Pentagon or the State Department, was already at work on a major Vietnam speech. The final version was Mr. Johnson's address to the nation on Sunday, March 31.

The speech was originally conceived late in February on the basis of Mr. Rostow's analysis that the Tet offensive had not been a real setback and that the allies should pull up their socks and hang on until the enemy came to his senses. While the discussions of troop strength were proceeding, Mr. McPherson was developing his draft.

Initially, it included an opened-ended commitment to the war—a willingness to carry on at whatever the cost. But as the internal debate over troop figures raged on and the numbers dwindled, the tone softened. But the President would not commit himself to any draft or any figure.

THE MARCH OF EVENTS

Then came a series of signal events: Senator Eugene J. McCarthy scored a stunning upset in the New Hampshire Democratic primary on March 1. American dead and wounded in Vietnam reached 139,801—exceeding over-all Korean-war losses. American and Western European bankers held an emergency meeting in Washington to stem the run of gold as the price soared. Senator Robert F. Kennedy announced on March 16 that he would seek the Democratic Presidential nomination.

All this formed the backdrop for the most delicate argument of all—that about the bombing.

On March 15, Arthur J. Goldberg, the American representative at the United Nations, sent an eight-page memo to the President urging him to halt the bombing to get negotiations started.

Others in the Administration favored such a step—Mr. Katzenbach and Ambassador-at-Large W. Averell Harriman, among them—but it was Ambassador Goldberg, increasingly frustrated by his sense of powerlessness on the Vietnam issue, who dared brook the President's anger by raising the issue directly.

Advisers like Mr. Rostow opposed a halt, maintaining that it would look like a sign of weakness and would undermine the confidence of the Saigon regime. The military insisted that it would jeopardize American troops just south of the demilitarized zone.

Still others, including Assistant Secretary of State Bundy, favored waiting for several weeks on the ground that another enemy offensive might be near.

A day after the Goldberg memo arrived, the subject came up in Mr. Johnson's inner circle. The President, his patience sorely tested, sat up in his chair and said:

"Let's get one thing clear! I'm telling you now I am not going to stop the bombing. Now I don't want to hear any more about it. Goldberg has written me about the whole thing, and I've heard every argument. I'm not going to stop it. Now is there anybody here who doesn't understand that?"

There was dead silence.

The bombing issue was dropped at that meeting, but it was not dead. Mr. Clifford, the lawyer, had noticed a loophole.

THE VIETNAM POLICY REVERSAL OF 1968: PART II

If ever there was a demonstration that no decision in Washington is final and that the struggle for a President's mind never really ends while he remains in office, it came a year ago this month.

"Let's get one thing clear!" President Johnson said forcefully to his Vietnam advisers on March 16, 1968. "I'm telling you now I am not going to stop the bombing. Now is there anybody here who doesn't understand that?"

No one misunderstood. The gathering in the gold and white Cabinet Room of the White House fell silent—but only temporarily. The dissenters from existing policy on Vietnam, who for two weeks had been battling against a request for massive troop reinforcements, chose to understand the President's pronouncement quite literally. They shifted tactics, and the argument flared up again.

In the Administration, Secretary of Defense Clark M. Clifford, who had entered the Government March 1 as a moderate hawk but was now an active dissident, took the initiative. He proposed that the bombing be restricted to the Panhandle region of North Vietnam south of the 20th Parallel.

No one knew where Mr. Johnson stood on that issue. It was still two weeks before he would announce a major shift in the direction of his Vietnam policy—a shift toward de-escalation that is still having its impact on the daily decisions of the Nixon Administration.

At that time the pressures for change—political and economic—were mounting. The public was increasingly impatient with the war.

"Something had to be done to extend the lease on public support for the war," a high State Department official remarked. "We were focused on what we could do without significant military drawbacks to make clear to people we were serious about peace."

Secretary Clifford pleaded skillfully for the proposal that the bombing be restricted to the region south of the 20th Parallel. A cutback, he said, would not violate the President's insistence that there be no halt without matching restraint from Hanoi. He added that it would not, as the military feared in the case of a halt, jeopardize American troops in outposts just south of the demilitarized zone—Khesanh, Camp Carroll, the Rockpile and others.

The region south of the 20th Parallel contains many of the "meatiest" targets. All North Vietnamese troops and most of the supplies heading into South Vietnam have to pass through this region.

The proposal was also thought to offer a diplomatic opening: If Hanoi and Washington were not able to walk directly to the negotiating table, Mr. Clifford suggested, perhaps they could begin to "crawl."

This was not a new idea. In the spring of 1967, Mr. Clifford's predecessor as Defense Secretary, Robert S. McNamara, had his aides draft a similar proposal for cutting back to the 19th or 20th Parallel as a means of starting the process of tacit de-escalation. For many months, too, Secretary of State Dean Rusk had been developing a variety of plans for cutbacks.

The theory was that if Washington made the first move, Hanoi might match it and, step by step, they could begin scaling down the war even without negotiations.

President Johnson refused to accept the plan after it ran into heavy opposition from the Joint Chiefs of staff. There were reports at the time that some senior generals would have resigned if it had been carried out.

Nonetheless, gingerly and indirect soundings of Hanoi were made at the time through what one diplomatic source called a "quasi-disavowable channel." The reaction from Hanoi, as read in Washington, was negative: Only a halt could produce talks. (The talks began in May, as it turned out, but the bombing did not come to a complete end until Nov. 1.)

Now, in March, 1968, the diplomatic experts thought that this was still a problem. Privately, the President had made no decision on the plan but publicly he was as stern as ever.

PRESIDENT DERIDES CRITICS

With Senator Robert F. Kennedy now in the race for the Democratic Presidential nomination and with the political tide apparently running against Mr. Johnson, he lashed back at his critics. In one of his pet phrases, he was "hunkering down like a Texas jackrabbit in a hailstorm."

On March 18 in Minneapolis, the President derided critics who would "tuck our tails and violate our commitments" in Vietnam. He raised the specter of appeasement in the Munich style. The Clifford camp took this as a counterattack aimed at them by the hawkish faction of the Administration led by Walt W. Rostow, the President's adviser on national security affairs.

President Johnson ridiculed proposals for shifting to a less ambitious ground strategy in Vietnam, as the doves wanted. "Those of you who think you can save lives by moving the battlefield in from the mountains to the cities where the people live have another think coming," he said acidly.

That remark in a speech and two more addresses in a similar tone discouraged the doves. Mr. Clifford, exhausted by his first two intensive weeks in office—during which he was directing the reappraisal of policy on the war—and suffering renewed complications from a case of hepatitis picked up in Vietnam the year before, felt that he had lost the argument.

The bombing cutback seemed to have been brushed aside. The only hopeful sign, Mr. Clifford thought, was the fact that Mr. Johnson had still not approved the troop reinforcements for Gen. William C. Westmoreland. The request by the American commander in Vietnam, which amounted to 206,000 men, had precipitated the reappraisal when presented by Gen. Earle G. Wheeler, Chairman of the Joint Chiefs of Staff, on Feb. 28.

It was clear in the middle of March that despite his public declarations, President Johnson was deeply uneasy and undecided.

GOLDBERG CALLS AT WHITE HOUSE

Late in the afternoon of March 20 he met in his oval office with Arthur J. Goldberg, the United States representative at the United Nations. It was their first meeting since Ambassador Goldberg, in a secret memo to the President on March 15, had proposed a bombing halt.

It was this proposal that had provoked the President's angry outburst at the White House meeting a day later. Mr. Goldberg had not been there and was unaware of Mr. Johnson's reaction. Now the two men met alone, and the President seemed interested in Ambassador Goldberg's position. He asked him to go through his arguments again, listening carefully and putting questions now and then. There were no angry words.

Before they parted, Mr. Johnson invited the silver-haired envoy to take part in a secret council of "wise men" that was to meet in Washington March 25. "I hope you'll put these same views to them there," he said.

The next hint of the President's thinking—though its significance was denied at the time—came on March 22. He announced that he was making General Westmoreland Army Chief of Staff, effective in July. He insisted that this did not necessarily foreshadow a change in strategy.

The White House explanation was that the shift had been in the mill for weeks and that the President was rewarding the general with the best job he could give him.

President Johnson was upset over the immediate speculation that, as an aide put it, he was "sacking Westy because of Tet," the costly Lunar New Year offensive the enemy had sprung in Vietnam on Jan. 30. To this day Mr. Johnson says privately as well as publicly that in his own heart that was not his motive. But some who know Lyndon Johnson extremely well believe that the shift came at this time—subconsciously, at least—as part of a gradual transition to a new policy.

Unknown to his political advisers, President Johnson was moving to settle the troop issue. He ordered General Wheeler to hold a secret rendezvous in the Pacific with General Westmoreland to learn if massive reinforcements were still needed. On March 24 the generals met alone for 90 minutes in 13th Air Force headquarters at Clark Air Force Base, in the Philippines.

General Westmoreland reported that the battlefield situation had improved—the crisis around the isolated Marine garrison at Khesanh had eased, the enemy seemed to have run out of steam and the South Vietnamese military forces were rebuilding their depleted ranks and moving back into the countryside.

Considering this trend, General Westmoreland said he would be satisfied if he could keep the two 5,000-man brigades rushed to Saigon early in February, at the peak of the enemy offensive, and if he were also given about 13,500 support troops for them.

General Wheeler flew back to report to the President, General Westmoreland sent a follow-up summary of his needs on March 28, three days before the President was to address the nation. No one was informed of the Pacific meeting.

By March 22, the inner circle in Washington had been informed that the President was going to give a Vietnam speech and they gathered in the family dining room of the White House to discuss it.

Present were the men who had shared the agony of Vietnam decisions with President Johnson—Secretary Rusk, Secretary Clifford, General Wheeler, press secretary, and Harry McPherson, a speech-writer.

The speech, conceived in the combative spirit after the Tet offensive, was still militant in tone. It deeply disturbed Mr. Clifford and others, who yearned to include some gesture of peace along with the scheduled reinforcements.

Once again Mr. Clifford urged the President to consider a bombing cutback on the ground that it would improve the Administration's position, internationally and domestically. Just two weeks before the crucial Democratic primary in Wisconsin, on April 2, most of the President's aides thought he needed a political shot in the arm. Vice President Humphrey believed that the bombing should be halted, not curtailed, if there was to be a change.

DOVES STILL TRYING

The discussion was exhaustive. How would a cutback affect Saigon? Would a bombing limitation to the 20th Parallel satisfy Hanoi? Were there other partial measures that made more sense?

After seven hours, Secretary Rusk gave a lucid summary. Mr. Rusk, who had himself raised the possibility of a bombing halt as early as March 3, said that there seemed to be a consensus that some step toward negotiations was desirable. But, according to one account, he cast doubt on whether a curtailment would satisfy the North Vietnamese.

"The feeling as we left," one participant recalled, "was that it would be nice if we could work it, but it wouldn't get anywhere."

The Administration doves had lost another round, but they did not relent.

The next morning Mr. McPherson, a bright, boyish-looking man, sent the President a memo that sought to strike a compromise between the general desire to make a peace gesture and the fear of rejection by Hanoi. The memo urged the President to stop the bombing north of the 20th Parallel and, simultaneously, to offer to stop the rest if Hanoi showed restraint at the demilitarized zone and left Saigon and other cities free from major attack.

The President sent the memo to Secretary Rusk, who later returned it with the comment that these were ideas that he had been working on and that they should be developed further. His reaction was favorable but, according to one account, he did not make any specific recommendation.

"WISE MEN" HAVE NEW THOUGHTS

Mr. Johnson also asked Mr. McPherson for another copy to send to Ambassador Ellsworth Bunker in Saigon. The answer that came back mentioned some of the problems Washington had anticipated but apparently did not raise any fundamental objections.

The time for decision was drawing near, but still the President hesitated.

"It was one of those periods when the President had everybody thinking he was about to make up his mind when actually he wasn't," a former White House official commented. "He has a facility for keeping his innermost thoughts to himself. He could keep everybody else lathered up the whole time. He just kept slipping back the deadlines for decision."

President Johnson, canvassing more opinion, was reaching outside the administration to summon to Washington the secret council of trusted advisers he mentioned to Ambassador Goldberg. They had a special and surprising impact on the President.

The previous fall, almost without exception and with Mr. Clifford a participant, they had backed the President's policy. But in the wake of the Tet offensive several of these influential men had had a change of heart.

Mr. Clifford, in his new role as an advocate of change and looking for allies, encouraged the President to call them into council again in the hope that it would strengthen his argument.

They gathered at the State Department on Monday, March 25, with the President's address to the nation six days away. They constituted a "who's who" of the American foreign-policy establishment:

Dean Acheson, Secretary of State under President Truman; George W. Ball, Under Secretary of State in the Kennedy and Johnson Administrations; Gen. Omar N. Bradley, retired World War II commander; McGeorge Bundy, special assistant for national security affairs to Presidents Kennedy and Johnson; Arthur H. Dean, President Eisenhower's Korean war negotiator; Douglas Dillon, Secretary of the Treasury under President Kennedy.

Also Associate Justice Abe Fortas of the Supreme Court; Mr. Goldberg;

Henry Cabot Lodge, twice Ambassador to Saigon; John J. McCloy, United States High Commissioner in West Germany under President Truman; Robert D. Murphy, ranking diplomat in the Truman-Eisenhower era; Gen. Matthew B. Ridgway, retired Korean war commander; Gen. Maxwell D. Taylor, former Chairman of the Joint Chiefs of Staff and a constant Presidential adviser on Vietnam, and Cyrus R. Vance, former Deputy Defense Secretary and President Johnson's trouble-shooter.

SOME PESSIMISM IS VOICED

The wise men heard candid briefings, some of which bordered on pessimism, and then questioned Messrs. Rusk, Clifford and Rostow and others about the extent of the Tet disaster and the plans for the future. The discussion continued late that night and resumed the next morning at the White House.

For the first time President Johnson got the trend of their views. He was "deeply shaken," one aide said, by the change of temper of the wise men, who were deeply discouraged over the war after the exalted hopes of the previous fall.

The President was especially impressed by the fact that Mr. Acheson, McGeorge Bundy and to a lesser degree Mr. Vance had joined Mr. Ball and Mr. Goldberg in opposing further military commitments and advocating some way of getting out of the war. He was jolted when Mr. Bundy, one of the architects of intervention in the early sixties and of the bombing of North Vietnam in 1965, now took an opposite tack.

There was, to be sure, a faction that held firm in defense of the harder line—Justice Fortas, General Taylor and Mr. Murphy. Mr. Murphy wanted more bombing, not less.

Ambassador Lodge, now President Nixon's chief negotiator in Paris, left the other participants puzzled. Several found him hawkish, but at least one said he was "on all sides of the issue." Mr. McCloy leaned toward the hawkish group.

Mr. Dean, Mr. Dillon and Generals Bradley and Ridgway were now doubters. They were plainly war-weary if not yet ready to shift course dramatically. The waning public support of the war was a constant concern.

There was no consensus on the bombing issue. Mr. Goldberg and Mr. Ball advocated a halt as a way to negotiations. The others were uncertain but the impression left with Government sources was that the wise men as a group were saying: "We had better start looking for another way to get this war settled."

THE PRIMARY WAS SECONDARY

To the President and his senior advisers, one close observer said later, such shifts carried "more weight than something like the New Hampshire primary." Someone suggested that Mr. Johnson consider the impact of his Vietnam decisions on the coming election; he replied testily that the campaign was the least of his concerns.

Two days later, on March 28, Messrs. Rusk, Clifford, Rostow, McPherson and William Bundy met in Mr. Rusk's mahogany-paneled office on the seventh floor of the State Department to polish the President's speech.

It was still, in the words of one participant, a "teeth-clenched, see-it-through" speech, announcing that about 15,000 more troops would be sent to Vietnam. It made a pro-forma plea for peace at the negotiating table and said nothing about cutting back the bombing.

Secretary Clifford launched an impassioned plea against taking this approach.

"I can't do it—I can't go along with it," he said. "I can't be in the position of trying to polish a speech of this kind. This speech can't be polished. What's needed is a new speech. This one is irrevocably setting the President down the wrong road."

The others listened as he spoke for nearly an hour, using to enormous advantage his almost unique position of being able to speak for the views of many outside.

It would tear the country apart, the Defense Secretary argued, to hear a speech that promised only more war. What was needed, he said, was not a "war speech, but a peace speech—the issue is as sharp as the edge of an ax."

To Mr. Clifford's surprise, Mr. Rusk did not cut him short. The others chimed in. Mr. Rusk sent out for sandwiches. Mr. Clifford appealed for some compromise, and once again they debated the 20th Parallel idea.

By this time the military commanders were no longer raising strong objections. Some, like Adm. U.S. Grant Sharp, the Pacific Fleet commander, who had over-all charge of the bombing, thought the cutback would fail. He fully expected that if it were tried, the President would order full bombing again in a month or so. Some officials thought this was Mr. Rostow's view also.

RUSK SWAYED BY THE DEBATE

Secretary Rusk, eager to find some way to the negotiating table, still did not think the cutback would satisfy Hanoi. The month's arguments had had a cumulative effect on him.

At the end of the day—the meeting lasted until 5 P.M.—Mr. Rusk had agreed with Mr. Clifford that Mr. McPherson should prepare "an alternate draft." That night, while the President was showing Senator Mike Mansfield, the Democratic majority leader, a draft of the original hawkish speech, Mr. McPherson began writing alternate draft No. 1. Working through the night, he had it ready by morning.

He sent the draft, the first one containing the proposal for a bombing cutback to the 20th Parallel, to Mr. Johnson with a note saying that it seemed to reflect the sentiments of some of the President's leading advisers. He also offered to go back to the original version if that was Mr. Johnson's wish.

Later in the day the President called Mr. McPherson in to discuss changes in an item on "Page 3." He did not specify which draft, but it was clear that he was now working with the new speech. That was how he signaled a major break in the debate.

He had been deeply influenced by the shift in the public mood, as reflected in the wise men's meetings and his contacts on Capitol Hill. The country was in turmoil and the dollar was in danger.

He had been shaken by the change in his old friend, Mr. Clifford, and was finally persuaded to try a new tack by Mr. Clifford's sheer persistence. The mood of others had softened in the crucible of debate, too.

FIVE MORE DRAFTS OF SPEECH

From then until 9 P.M. on the 31st, the speech went through five more drafts. None changed the new essence, though there was one important tug-of-war over the wording on the bombing cutback.

Under Secretary of State Nicholas B. Katzenbach, drawn into the top-level discussions since Secretary Rusk was leaving for a Pacific meeting with the Vietnam allies, opposed naming the 20th Parallel as the cutoff point.

Mr. Katzenbach had long favored a halt. Now he wanted the northern limit to be the 19th Parallel rather than the 20th, but the military insisted on the 20th so they could hit Thanhhoa, a railroad-switching point, and Route 7, leading into Laos—both just south of the 20th Parallel.

The Under Secretary, who suggested that it not be stated so baldly, was looking for a way to "winch" the limit further southward. And, like most Administration officials, he was operating under the mistaken assumption that one main purpose of the speech was to help President Johnson in the April 2 Democratic primary in Wisconsin.

Suggesting that the speech would have more public appeal if it emphasized that part of the bombing would be continued to protect American troops just south of the demilitarized zone, Mr. Katzenbach drafted a revision that said all bombing should stop "except in an area north of the demilitarized zone where the continuing enemy buildup directly threatens allied forward positions." His amendment specified that this would spare almost 90 percent of North Vietnam's population.

ROSTOW PHONES KATZENBACH

The President liked that language and accepted it. On Saturday he asked Mr. Rostow to telephone Mr. Katzenbach, now Acting Secretary, to persuade him to accept the 20th Parallel as the northern limit.

Reluctantly Mr. Katzenbach agreed, but with a caveat: "Don't make the first big raid at 19 degrees 59 minutes. Make sure the orders are consistent with the speech." Mr. Rostow replied that this would be done.

But they had different interpretations of what they had agreed on. Mr. Katzenbach thought he had won agreement on a plan that would let the bombing "roll northward" gradually from the buffer area as battlefield conditions dictated. Mr. Rostow felt he had Mr. Katzenbach's approval for military orders saying simply that bombing north of the 20th Parallel was forbidden after March 31.

On the Saturday a small group worked with President Johnson, who was in good spirits going over the text line by line until about 9 P.M. The speech had become progressively more dovish until, one official said, "it ended up 180 degrees from where it started."

Late the previous day Mr. Clifford had been concerned that the peroration, left over from original drafts, was still too militant, so Mr. McPherson was to draft a substitute.

When the Saturday session ended Mr. Johnson asked for the revised peroration. Mr. McPherson said he had not had time to rewrite it but would do so promptly.

"I MAY HAVE ONE OF MY OWN"

The President, his shirt open and his tie down, muttered, "No need to—I may have one of my own." He winked at Mr. McPherson, who turned to Mr. Clifford and said: "My God? Do you think he is going to say sayonara?" Mr. Clifford responded with a strange and unbelieving grimace.

On Sunday the President had Horace Busby, another speech-writer, and Mr. Christian working on the withdrawal section. Mr. McPherson, still officially in the dark on the President's political plans, assumed that he did not want his ending.

But Mr. Johnson kept sending word that he did indeed want Mr. McPherson's peroration, obviously intending to deliver both.

Initially Mr. Johnson hesitated to make his withdrawal announcement with the policy declaration. But sometime near the end of March, as he became convinced of the need for a bombing cutback, he evidently concluded that it would be more effective if he made it clear that he was not just appealing for votes or pacifying domestic critics or serving some other personal interest.

The approach of the Wisconsin primary also served as a deadline for action, in the view of some of his political advisers. They thought his withdrawal would be more dignified and more effective if made before the primary rather than after the expected victory for Senator Eugene J. McCarthy of Minnesota.

By the eve of the speech the President's mind was made up.

He did not sleep particularly well that night, and he was up before dawn. In the afternoon, he began rehearsing the Vietnam portion of the speech. About 4 P.M. Mr. Busby gave him the revised ending on not seeking re-election. The President made a few final adjustments to insure that his motives would be understood.

At 8 P.M. the text was turned over to an Army Signal Corps man to put on prompter devices, and the President told his aides to begin informing members of the Cabinet of his intentions.

Secretary Clifford and his wife were invited to the Executive Mansion half an hour before the President was to go on nationwide television. Mr. Clifford already knew of the Vietnam decision—the bombing cutback to the 20th Parallel, 13,500 more troops for General Westmoreland and more equipment for the South Vietnamese Army at a cost of $2.5 billion a year.

After the wrenching tensions of the policy debate and the chill that had crept into their personal relations, the Secretary was warmed to learn that the President wanted to see him before delivering the speech. Upstairs in the family quarters, the Cliffords joined Mrs. Johnson and Jack Valenti, the President's former aide and an old Texas friend.

Mr. Johnson motioned Mr. Clifford into his bedroom and without a word handed him the last two paragraphs of the speech.

"With America's sons in the fields far away, with America's future under challenge right here at home, with our hopes and the world's hopes for peace in the balance every day," the President told the nation later, "I do not believe that I should devote an hour or a day of my time to any personal, partisan causes or to any duties other than the awesome duties of this office—the Presidency of your country.

"Accordingly, I shall not seek, and I will not accept, the nomination of my party for another term as your President."

EPILOGUE

The President's speech brought Washington—and the nation—the relief it feels when a breezy summer day breaks a sweltering heat wave. The bitterness of months had been lanced in a stroke. There was a rare moment of harmony. But it was only an instant.

Within 36 hours, while the world awaited Hanoi's response, Navy jets struck Thanhhoa, 210 miles north of the demilitarized zone, the very kind of raid that Mr. Katzenbach had wanted to prevent.

The enormous relief evaporated. The heat wave was back. The politicians, not knowing that the Russians and Hanoi had been privately told that the northern limit of the bombing was the 20th Parallel, complained that the public had been misled. State Department officials privately accused the military commanders of trying to sabotage the President's peace initiative.

With a new political storm mounting, Mr. Clifford persuaded President Johnson to pull the bombing back to the 19th Parallel on the pretext that some American planes might have strayed over the 20th Parallel. It was a decision that Mr. Rostow, General Wheeler, General Westmoreland and others tried many times to reverse.

And so it went—all summer, all fall—the two coalitions in the Administration battling for the President's favor. "It was like climbing the greasy pole," recalled an insider. "You wanted to continue climbing higher but you had to keep fighting to stay where you were."

In May, the hawks were urging escalation after enemy forces had launched their mini-Tet offensive.

General Westmoreland also wanted approval to launch B-52 raids and small ground forays against enemy supply dumps and base camps in remote areas of Cambodia, when enemy forces pulled back to these sanctuaries from assaults on American outposts. But President Johnson rejected this plan firmly.

In June, when enemy rockets were falling on Saigon, Ambassador Ellsworth Bunker was privately urging that the United States retaliate by bombing Hanoi. One official said the United States was "within two days" of stepping up the bombing of North Vietnam when the attacks on Saigon stopped.

Next it was the doves. During the prolonged summer battlefield lull W. Averell Harriman and Cyrus R. Vance, the American negotiators in Paris, tried to talk the President into a total bombing halt.

They made their pitch at the end of July. It was strictly a ploy. They accepted the military estimate that the lull was not deliberate and that the enemy was merely regrouping and refitting his forces. But they suggested that President Johnson treat it as deliberate restraint anyway.

The proposal was to tell Hanoi that since it had de-escalated the war, the United States would end the bombing, but that to sustain this cessation, Hanoi would have to refrain from another offensive. The hope was to talk Hanoi into restraint.

Mr. Clifford and Vice President Humphrey promoted the idea. Mr. Katzenbach and Mr. Bundy were in Paris at this time, and simultaneously, The New York Times in a July 29 editorial advocated a similar tactic.

It was all too much for President Johnson. "He thought it was conspiracy," said one high official. "There were so many coincidences that he thought it stank to high heaven." He rejected the plan out of hand.

In October, as in March, there was another debate. To all the complications of the earlier argument were added the intricacies—and miscalculations—of dealing with the South Vietnamese. Finally, on Oct. 31, the President stopped all the bombing of North Vietnam but even that did not stop the inner wrangling.

The struggle for the President's mind persisted until the day he left office.

Appendix II

Presidential Decision-making: President Nixon
To Invade Cambodia

President Nixon's venture into Cambodia is ending with proclamations of unprecedented military gain, but it was launched for the broader purpose of rescuing Cambodia from sudden Communist domination and that purpose is still unrealized.

A reconstruction shows that the survival of an anti-Communist Government in Cambodia came to be seen by Mr. Nixon as essential for the defense of Vietnam and the American stake in Indochina. As pieced together by correspondents of *The New York Times* in Washington, Saigon and Pnompenh, Mr. Nixon's handling of his most serious crisis also involved the following main factors:

The President, believing that Communist nations had long been trifling with him in Indochina, Korea and the Middle East, saw Cambodia as the first feasible opportunity to demonstrate that he could meet force with force.

Mr. Nixon was haunted by intelligence reports that enemy commanders were moving against Cambodia, confident that American hands were tied by war-weariness at home.

Before attacking, the Nixon Administration tried to signal circuitously to Hanoi that it would accept an accommodation—which the Cambodian Government was seeking—provided that Cambodia's principal port remained closed to Communist supply shipments. The overtures collapsed over the port issue.

This Appendix reprints an article originally published in *The New York Times* of June 30, 1970. It was written by Hedrick Smith in collaboration with Max Frankel, and incorporates reports by William Beecher, Henry Giniger, Henry Kamm, Sydney H. Schanberg, Robert B. Semple Jr., Neil Sheehan, Terence Smith, James P. Sterba and Tad Szulc. Copyright © 1970 by The New York Times Company. Reprinted by permission.

Once he felt himself militarily challenged by the enemy in Cambodia, Mr. Nixon pushed the pace of decision-making here—so much that one senior adviser cautioned him that the generals in Saigon might be giving the President only the advice they thought he wanted to hear.

Repeated and forceful opposition to the use of American troops in Cambodia from Secretary of State William P. Rogers, stressing the risks of domestic discontent, caused Mr. Nixon to delay the operation 24 hours.

Once decided, Mr. Nixon also ordered four heavy bombing raids against North Vietnam, despite the year-and-a-half-old cessation of United States raids on the North—with the purpose, officials now acknowledge, of warning Hanoi against counterattacking across the demilitarized zone into South Vietnam. The four attacks appeared to be a violation of the private understandings with Hanoi prohibiting bombing of the North.

LIKE PREDECESSORS, UNEASY

Formally, the Cambodian operations began with a Presidential announcement on April 30. But for Mr. Nixon, the beginning was well before that.

Like President Kennedy in the Cuban crisis and President Johnson in Vietnam, he felt Communist forces crowding and testing him. He had contained the frustration of not retaliating when the North Vietnamese shelled Saigon early in his term, when North Korea shot down an American intelligence plane, when the Paris peace talks bogged down. Now the Soviet Union was moving combat pilots into the United Arab Republic and Communist forces were threatening another nation in Indochina.

Of all these situations, Mr. Nixon felt, Cambodia offered the first opening for effective military reaction that would carry his larger political message. As the President confided to a senior adviser: This is a risk, but this is the kind of thing he had been waiting for.

Mr. Nixon's objectives in Cambodia centered on staving off Communist domination. Survival of Premier Lon Nol's Government, for a time, at least, appeared essential. Its survival was needed to assure the defense of South Vietnam and the process of American withdrawal, to spare Saigon the blow of seeing a neighbor collapse while the United States did nothing and to deny Hanoi a gain that would tempt it, in the words of one senior adviser, to "go for all the marbles" in Indochina and forever spurn negotiation.

LIFT FOR THE PREMIER

An American attack from the rear, Mr. Nixon thought, would divert and disrupt the enemy forces threatening General Lon Nol and also give the Cambodian Premier a badly needed political lift. But it required no open commitment.

Despite his preference for orderly procedure, President Nixon, like his predecessors, reacted in crisis with rump-group meetings, late phone calls, an out-of-channel message to the field and other activities that bypassed planners at the State and Defense Departments.

The White House became so worried about security leaks that even members of the Joint Chiefs of Staff were late to learn some critical discussions. State Department lawyers were not told to prepare the legal case for invasion until four days after it began.

The gestation process for Mr. Nixon's decision was much longer than Administration accounts suggested. It began almost immediately after General Lon Nol and others deposed Prince Norodom Sihanouk on March 18.

TWILIGHT ZONE OF WAR

For years, Cambodia was a twilight zone of the Vietnam war. Prince Sihanouk, balancing between the belligerents, had let the North Vietnamese create a dozen base areas to shelter 40,000 to 60,000 troops for use against South Vietnam.

American generals had periodically pressed the Johnson Administration for permission to attack these sanctuaries, but President Johnson had refused. The Nixon Administration grudgingly tolerated the situation. Its plans for a gradual troop withdrawal from Vietnam assumed that the enemy bases in Cambodia would remain intact.

Within the last year, however, even Prince Sihanouk began to worry about the expanding enemy activity on his soil. He allowed American B-52's to bomb the base areas. For a time, he curtailed the enemy supply shipments to the bases through the port, then Sihanoukville, now Kompong Som.

Prince Sihanouk's ouster, described as a surprise in Washington, posed an opportunity. All foreign-policy agencies quickly drafted proposals for dealing with the new situation. In this process, Secretary of Defense Melvin R. Laird invited the generals in Saigon to submit contingency plans.

ABRAMS'S OPTIONS

By April 1, Gen. Creighton W. Abrams, the United States commander in Vietnam had offered the Pentagon several options:

First, to let South Vietnamese troops harass the enemy across the border.

Second, to help the South Vietnamese Army conduct larger attacks over a period of months to disrupt the enemy bases.

Or third, to let American forces join the South Vietnamese in a swift full-scale assault on the bases.

Using the American forces was the "top option" but General Abrams did not formally recommend any course.

Washington was still looking for diplomatic ways to contain the Cambodian situation. Perhaps Hanoi, with its forces now less secure in Cambodia, would show interest in negotiation—if not on Vietnam alone then in the context of an international conference on all Indochina, which France proposed on April 1.

General Lon Nol tried to work out live-and-let-live arrangements with the North Vietnamese, first in direct talks and then through Chinese and other Communist intermediaries. He asked North Vietnam to reduce its military presence in Cambodia and its reliance on shipments through Sihanoukville. Hanoi refused.

Washington made no direct approach to Hanoi, but passed word to Asian intermediaries that it would respect any deal General Lon Nol made. It got no diplomatic reply.

ONE DIPLOMAT UNSURE

One diplomat said the American approach was so feeble and casual that he was not sure the intermediaries understood that the messages were meant for Hanoi. American officials, moreover, were sure that Hanoi suspected the United States of having ousted Prince Sihanouk and could not, therefore, credit Washington with good faith.

South Vietnamese forces, meanwhile, were staging sporadic raids across the Cambodian border, against the advice of American officials in Saigon. The United States increased bombing raids against enemy concentrations in Cambodia, but General Abrams's contingency plans, now sent by the Joint Chiefs of Staff to the White House, were in limbo. Secretary Laird, talking with President Nixon in the second week of April, opposed an American assault because he feared heavy casualties—as high as 400 to 800 dead in the first week alone—and a public outcry.

MOVEMENTS WESTWARD

In mid-April the combat situation changed. Starting April 13, enemy forces were detected moving westward into Cambodia from the border areas, cutting roads, blowing up bridges, harassing military posts and towns. The White House interpreted the reports "leniently"—as reliable on the location of enemy actions, but not on their size, seriousness or intent.

In Saigon, however, General Abrams was particularly struck by the thinning out of enemy forces in the Fishhook, a Cambodian salient that juts into South Vietnam 75 miles northwest of Saigon. The Fishhook was considered the most important enemy refuge area.

General Abrams and Ellsworth Bunker, the American Ambassador, met privately for several nights and about April 15, sent parallel recommendations to the Departments of State and Defense. They urged an American attack into the Fishhook and joint attacks with the South Vietnamese against other bases.

ARGUMENTS SUMMARIZED

High military sources summed up General Abrams's arguments as follows:

One of the two American divisions standing guard against attacks from the enemy bases in Cambodia was going home soon under President Nixon's withdrawal program, shifting a major burden to Saigon's forces. With the rainy season approaching and the Lon Nol Government unlikely to survive until fall, the time was right. An attack would help the South Vietnamese and assure further American withdrawals. With a third of the enemy forces moved west, the risks of American casualties were reduced.

The general's argument, envisioning benefits for the Vietnamization program, impressed Secretary Laird. The promise of lower casualties convinced him, and he endorsed the proposal.

But at the White House, the military possibilities were still offset by the fear of pushing the war deeper into Cambodia and the fear of spoiling the chances for negotiation.

The prospects for diplomacy had unexpectedly improved when the Soviet Union said that it, too, was interested in an Indochina conference. "Only a new Geneva conference could bring a new solution and relax tension," Yakov A. Malik, the Soviet representative at the United Nations, said on April 16. The Americans got private indications that this was a deliberate initiative and assumed that the Russians had cleared it with Hanoi.

PRESSURES STILL RISE

Still, the pressures in Cambodia were building up. Premier Lon Nol pleaded with greater urgency each day. Mr. Nixon did not want another state in Southeast Asia dependent on the United States, but neither did he want to stand idly by. High officials felt the whole rationale for defending South Vietnam would collapse if they acquiesced in a Communist take-over of Laos and Combodia. Also, the President feared Prince Sihanouk, with Hanoi's aid, might be returned to power.

So Mr. Nixon set out to help Premier Lon Nol clandestinely. He let Saigon's forces increase the scope and frequency of their attacks into Cambodia. The purpose, one high official said later, was "to put pressure on the enemy forces so they wouldn't turn toward Pnompenh."

American advisers were told to help plan the enlarged raids, but not get into combat inside Cambodia.

By April 17, the President had also approved a secret shipment of 6,000 captured AK-47 rifles of Soviet design to the Cambodian Army. The United States first tried to use Indonesia as a cover for this aid, but for reasons of diplomacy, shifted to South Vietnam.

Plans were also made to assemble a force of 2,000 Khmer Krom troops to stiffen the Cambodian army. These mercenaries fighting in South Vietnam for the American Special Forces were later flown secretly to Pnompenh.

PRESIDENT DISTRACTED

President Nixon evidently hoped that these measures would win time. He was, in any case, distracted by the battle over his Supreme Court nominees, the Apollo 13 astronauts and the need to announce another troop withdrawal.

General Abrams was pleading for a 60-day delay in withdrawals. Secretary Laird wanted a cutback of 50,000 by Aug. 15. With the issue unresolved, Mr. Nixon went to greet the returning astronauts in Honolulu.

He finally hit on a compromise, surprising even some senior advisers: to delay withdrawals for 60 days but to hide that fact in an announcement of a full year's pullouts—150,000 men by May, 1971. Mr. Nixon flew back to San Clemente, Calif., to make the announcement April 20—a long and, as it turned out, fateful day in his perception of the situation in Indochina.

The speech emphasized his terms for a political settlement in more flexible terms than ever before.

HE REITERATES WARNINGS

He did point with concern to "the enemy's escalation in Laos and Cambodia" and repeated warnings that if "increased enemy action jeopardizes our remaining forces in Vietnam, I shall not hesitate to take strong and effective measures to deal with that situation."

There was no real hint of the internal discussions about Cambodia.

Officials insist that Mr. Nixon's optimism did not disguise any secret calculations. Press dispatches had already reported the fall of Saang, a district capital 18 miles from Pnompenh, but official confirmation did not reach the traveling White House until late on April 20.

On that day, too—although it was probably unknown to Mr. Nixon as he spoke—Hanoi's spokesman in Peking indicated that Prince Sihanouk was joining a new united military front for the "liberation" of all Indochina; the Russians backed off their interest in a Geneva conference, and the Lon Nol regime submitted a request for more than $500 million in military aid.

Mr. Nixon was restless that night—"wound up," his wife said—and after his speech, abruptly flew back to Washington. One aide said afterward that the President might have sensed "something was up."

CONFIRMED BY INTELLIGENCE

By morning, intelligence reports had built up a picture of steady deterioration in Cambodia, but the problem hit Mr. Nixon with sudden force.

From that day on, Mr. Nixon got daily briefings from Richard Helms, Director of Central Intelligence. Details were sketchy, but the Communists were attacking Saang, Takeo and Angtassom, south of Pnompenh and Snoul and Memot, to the north.

The State Department surmised that the enemy was using hit-and-run maneuvers to create an impression of civil war. The Pentagon view, more persuasive to the White House, was that the North Vietnamese had decided to overthrow Lon Nol by isolating his capital, or taking it.

Mr. Nixon summoned the National Security Council to meet on April 22, the group's first consideration of the contingency plans. The talk centered largely on a proposed South Vietnamese offensive into the Parrot's Beak, an enemy position jutting into Vietnam 35 miles from Saigon. There was some discussion of an American attack into the Fishhook.

CRISIS SCHEDULE ENFORCED

The next morning, the President seemed bent on some kind of action. He called for operational plans for the Parrot's Beak, forcing a crisis schedule upon the Washington Special Action Group—a body headed by Henry A. Kissinger, his special assistant for security affairs.

The group, which is called WASAG, was created in April, 1969, when North Korea shot down an American intelligence plane. It played a central role in the Cambodian venture from late March onward by assembling and refining all contingency plans, assessing their consequence, and managing the execution of Presidential orders.

At the peak of crisis, the group's members were Mr. Kissinger; David Packard, Deputy Secretary of Defense; U. Alexis Johnson, Under Secretary of State for Political Affairs; Mr. Helms; Gen. Earle G. Wheeler, then Chairman of the Joint Chiefs; Adm. Thomas H. Moorer, his successor, and Marshall Green, Assistant Secretary of State for East Asian Affairs.

The group met twice on April 23, again on April 24. In Saigon, the South Vietnamese generals were hesitant about a major strike without the Americans. General Abrams and Ambassador Bunker met with President Nguyen Van Thieu, after which Saigon finally geared for action while General Abrams pressed Washington to use American advisers in the Parrot's Beak operation.

NIXON IS IRRITATER

Mr. Nixon was now pushing the process of making decisions, irritated that the enemy appeared complacent. American intelligence confirmed anew that the enemy command was telling its troops to push west without fear of an American attack from the rear. The White House denounced the enemy moves as a "foreign invasion."

On Friday morning, April 24, the President called for operational plans for the Fishhook operation to be delivered from Saigon within 24 hours. He called a secret meeting of the National Security Council for Sunday, pointing toward a final decision Sunday night. This would give the generals the 72 hours they said they needed to attack on April 29, which would be dawn, April 30, Saigon time.

The President flew to Camp David, Md., Friday afternoon. Mr. Kissinger brought the plans on Saturday and the two men studied them. In Washington that evening, they conferred with Secretary Laird and Attorney General John N. Mitchell aboard the Government yacht Sequoia on the Potomac. They then attended a private showing of "Patton," the film biography of the defiant general, which Mr. Nixon was eager to see for a second time.

TWO MEMBERS ABSENT

Secretary of State Rogers returned from New York on Sunday morning and, with Secretary Laird, heard a Pentagon briefing on the Fishhook plans. Thus all participants in the afternoon meeting of the Security Council were prepared for the main topic of debate.

The two Secretaries joined the President, the Attorney General, General Wheeler, Mr. Helms and Mr. Kissinger at the Executive Office Building next to the White House. Two statutory members of the Council, Vice President Agnew and George A. Lincoln, director of the Office of Emergency Preparedness, were not present.

Mr. Nixon said that he had decided "to do something." The Parrot's Beak operation had his tentative approval, with American ground advisers. The Fishhook was the problem at hand.

The Pentagon representatives argued that a full assault, with American troops, was essential. Military analysis showed the enemy seeking either to topple the Lon Nol regime or to clear a supply corridor to the sea in eastern Cambodia. Either prospect jeopardized the defense of South Vietnam and American withdrawal. The Parrot's Beak alone would serve only as a warning. Using the South Vietnamese in the Fishhook would require a major reshuffle of armies, and might prove too difficult for them. With the heavy rains due in a month, and Lon Nol unlikely to survive until fall, it was now or never.

Secretary Rogers carried the principal burden of opposition. The use of American troops in Cambodia meant widening the war. The risk was grave of becoming entrapped, as the Johnson Administration had been. The President won wide popular support for gradual withdrawal and should not risk losing it. The allies' military objectives could be achieved by South Vietnamese forces alone.

THEY MEET FOR THREE HOURS

The debate lasted three hours, ranging over other enemy base areas. Mr. Nixon came away thinking he had a choice of doing nothing or involving American troops. An attack in the Parrot's Beak alone seemed unlikely to bring much military advantage. To use only South Vietnamese ground forces would be a pretense, for American air and logistical support was deemed essential. It was a line of thinking Mr. Kissinger appears to have shared. Besides, the President was determined to prove that he could meet force with force.

Mr. Nixon withdrew to his hideaway office and ordered a tray of dinner. On a pad of yellow legal paper he summarized the pros and cons. As disclosed by Stewart Alsop in Newsweek and later confirmed officially, the President's doodling showed how intimately the survival of the Lon Nol regime had become linked in his mind with American success in Vietnam.

In reviewing whether there should be some action in Cambodia, Mr. Nixon listed only arguments in favor: "Time running out" was followed by "military aid" to Lon Nol could be "only symbolic." Then came a scribble saying inaction might tempt Hanoi to install a puppet regime in Pnompenh and a final entry saying that inaction by both sides would leave an "ambiguous situation" with time favoring the Communists.

LIABILITIES LISTED

The President then listed the pros and cons for American action in the Fishhook and for a South Vietnamese attack alone in the Parrot's Beak. He recognized that the Fishhook move would bring a "deep division" of the American people. He feared that it might provoke a collapse of the Paris talks, an attack on Pnompenh or a major North Vietnamese attack across the DMZ.

Mr. Nixon seemed determined to attack, but the opposing arguments of Secretary Rogers evidently led him to break his own deadline. He called another meeting for Monday morning, April 27, with Mr. Rogers, Mr. Laird, Mr. Kissinger and H. R. Haldeman, his chief of staff, but without the military or intelligence chiefs.

Someone—apparently still Mr. Rogers—suggested that the military might be telling the President only what it thought he wanted to hear. The suggestion haunted Mr. Nixon. Out of that meeting came his personal, out-of-channels message to General Abrams demanding "the unvarnished truth," man to man.

ABRAMS SEES NECESSITY

That afternoon, Mr. Rogers testified at a closed session of the Senate Foreign Relations Committee and ran into a storm of opposition to possible American involvement in Cambodia. Without directly disclosing the contemplated use of United States troops, he tried to hint at the imminence of a military decision. Mr. Rogers recounted the Senators' objections in a long telephone report to the President that evening.

From Saigon, General Abrams replied that an American assault was necessary. With that message and new memos from other advisers, and after one more call to Mr. Laird, Mr. Nixon withdrew to make his conveyed it, first to Mr. Kissinger and then to Mr. Rogers, Mr. Laird and Mr. Mitchell, whose advice, always important to the President, is not known in this case.

Having decided to attack in the Fishhook, the President said that he was also sending American ground advisers into the Parrot's Beak and ordering consecutive attacks on a number of enemy base areas. As the operation unfolded, he also approved the four raids on North Vietnam.

Ignoring some advice that he treat the event in a low key, the President prepared his own television address, working it through eight longhand drafts on Tuesday and Wednesday night, staying up to 5 A.M. Unlike Presidents Kennedy and Johnson, he never submitted it for editing by his main cabinet advisers. All of Mr. Nixon's senior aides still wince at some of his rhetoric.

Some of Mr. Nixon's senior aides, were troubled by the President's apocalyptic vision of the stakes. Others found some military points over-dramatized.

The President's assertion that the enemy was massing in the sanctuaries to attack South Vietnam contradicted Secretary Laird's support of the American assault because of the enemy's movement the other way. It also contradicted the latest intelligence that the enemy forces had sensed what was coming and were dispersing faster than before with some of their arms caches.

The generals felt uneasy that Mr. Nixon, to give importance to his move, led the American public to expect the capture of top enemy commanders by announcing an attack on "the headquarters for the entire Communist military operation in South Vietnam." They knew the enemy command unit—the Central Office for South Vietnam, called COSVN—was always on the move and doubted they would catch its 200 men in the Fishhook. Their troops were ordered to "neutralize the COSVN base area"—meaning arms caches, supply dumps and other facilities.

CABLE OFFICE CLOSED

Notice of the President's speech reached Premier Lon Nol only after it was over, because the Pnompenh cable office was closed. Although he had agreed in mid-April to deeper raids by the South Vietnamese and more recently to the Parrot's Beak operation, his consent was not sought for the Fishhook. The White House believed if he said "no," it was in trouble; if he said "yes," he might be.

In the days following Mr. Nixon's speech, what the Congress and the public took to be limitations of time and scope on the invasion were only firm definitions of the Administration's private intentions: six to eight weeks and a limit to penetrations of about 20 miles. Some field commanders even found the time limit a welcome surprise; they had expected two to four weeks.

But other rules of engagement had to be adjusted to the enemy's spreading attacks throughout Cambodia. To help Premier Lon Nol defend himself in the months ahead, the Administration agreed to leave South Vietnamese troops behind after June 30 and tried to arrange Thai support as well.

American planes now fly tactical air support for the Cambodians under the guise of raids against enemy supply lines. American ships blockade Cambodia's coastline. And new military and economic aid is being prepared. Thus, the operation, now formally ended is, in fact, far from over.

Selected Bibliography

The books and articles listed comprise a highly selective bibliography of available works on presidents and the presidency. There are many good general works which are not listed, but which can be easily found by going through the card catalogues and readers guides of any library. It is only those works which this author finds particularly valuable and/or intriguing which are included here.

A great many political scientists have written a great variety of books about the presidency, and only some of them are listed. While they do present a framework in which to view the presidency, they rarely manage to convey any real idea of how the White House operates on a day-to-day basis or what different administrations are like. For this kind of information, the student is well advised to turn to some of the books that have been written about specific presidents and their administrations. Most of the best books have been written either by members of the administrations or by journalists.

Students of the presidency who want to become knowledgeable must follow the activities of the president as they occur. There is absolutely no substitute for the information available to the White House press corps, or the kind of experienced analysis the best correspondents can turn out regularly. Such reporters as Tom Wicker and Robert B. Semple, Jr., of the *New York Times,* Mary McGrory of the *Washington Star,* Peter Lisagor of the *Chicago Daily News,* a number of correspondents for the *St. Louis Post-Dispatch* and the *Los Angeles Times,* Richard Rovere of the *New Yorker,* John Osborne of the *New Republic,* etc. can be far more illuminating about what is happening during any given moment in a presidency than any group of political scientists. At least one of them should be read regularly by anyone interested in the presidency.

On the assumption that most students are primarily interested in the post-Eisenhower presidents and that footnotes in later volumes can be followed back to worthwhile earlier ones, this bibliography includes only recent books and articles.

I. GENERAL WORKS

Barber, James David, ed. *Political Leadership in American Government*. Boston Little, Brown and Co., 1964.

Burns, James MacGregor. *Presidential Government: The Crucible of Leadership*. Boston: Houghton Mifflin Co., 1965.

Finer, Herman. *The Presidency: Crisis and Regeneration*. Chicago: University of Chicago Press, 1960.

Hargrove, Erwin Co. *Presidential Leadership: Personality and Political Style*. New York: Macmillan Co., 1966.

James, Dorothy Buckton. *The Contemporary Presidency*. New York: Pegasus (Publishers), 1969.

Keoning, Louis W. *The Chief Executive*. Revised edition. New York: Harcourt Brace Jovanovich, 1968.

McConnell, Grant. *The Modern Presidency*. New York: St. Martin's Press, 1967.

Neustadt, Richard E. *Presidential Power: The Politics of Leadership*. New York: John Wiley & Sons, 1960.

Polsby, Nelson W. *The President and Congress*. Englewood Cliffs, N.J.: Prentice-Hall, 1964.

Reedy, George E. *The Twilight of the Presidency*. New York: World Publishing Co., 1970.

Rossiter, Clinton. *The American Presidency*. New York: Harcourt Brace Jovanovich, 1960.

Wise, Sidney, and Schier, Richard F. *The Presidential Office*. Thomas Y. Crowell Co., 1968.

II. PRESIDENTS AND ADMINISTRATIONS

Anderson, Patrick. *The President's Men: White House Assistants of Franklin D. Roosevelt, Harry S Truman, Dwight D. Eisenhower, John F. Kennedy and Lyndon B. Johnson*. New York: Doubleday & Co., 1968.

Christian, George. *The President Steps Down*. New York: Macmillan Co., 1970.

Evans, Rowland, and Novak, Robert. *Lyndon B. Johnson: The Exercise of Power*. New York: New American Library, 1966.

Graff, Henry F. *The Tuesday Cabinet: Deliberation and Decision on Peace and War Under Lyndon B. Johnson*. Englewood Cliffs, N.J.: Prentice-Hall, 1970.

Harris, Richard. *Decision*. New York: E. P. Dutton & Co., 1971.

Heren, Louis. *No Hail, No Farewell*. New York: Harper & Row, Publishers, 1970.

Hilsman, Roger. *To Move a Nation: The Politics of Foreign Policy in the Administration of John F. Kennedy*. New York: Doubleday & Co., 1967.

Hoopes, Townsend. *The Limits of Intervention*. New York: David McKay Co., 1969.

Kennedy Robert F. *Thirteen Days: A Memoir of the Cuban Missile Crisis*. New York: W. W. Norton & Co., 1968.

Osborne, John. *The Nixon Watch*. New York: Liveright Publishing Corp., 1970.

——. *The Second Year of The Nixon Watch*. New York: Liveright Publishing Corp., 1971.

Schlesinger, Arthur M., Jr. *A Thousand Days: John F. Kennedy in the White House.* Boston: Houghton Mifflin Co., 1965.

Sidey, Hugh. *John F. Kennedy, President.* New York: Atheneum Publishers, Crest Books, 1963.

Sorensen, Theodore C. *Kennedy.* New York: Harper & Row Publishers, 1965.

Sundquist, James L. *Politics and Policy: The Eisenhower, Kennedy, and Johnson Years.* Washington, D.C.: Brookings Institution, 1968.

Wicker, Tom *JFK and LBJ: The Influence of Personality Upon Politics.* New York: William Morrow & Co., 1968.

III. ASPECTS OF THE PRESIDENCY

Brown, Stuart Gerry. *The American Presidency: Leadership, Partisanship, and Popularity.* New York: Macmillan Co., 1966.

Burns, James MacGregor. *The Deadlock of Democracy.* Englewood Cliffs, N.J.: Prentice-Hall, 1963.

Cambell, John Franklin. *The Foreign Affairs Fudge Factory.* New York: Basic Books, 1971.

Chester, Lewis; Hodgson, Godfrey; and Page, Bruce. *An American Melodrama: The Presidential Campaign of 1968.* New York: Viking Press, 1969.

Cornwell, Elmer E., Jr. *Presidential Leadership of Public Opinion.* Bloomington, Ind.: Indiana University Press, 1965.

Cronin, Thomas E., and Greenberg, Sanford D., eds. *The Presidential Advisory System.* New York: Harper & Row, Publishers, 1969.

David, Paul T.; Goldman; Ralph M.; and Baia, Richard D. *The Politics of National Party Conventions.* New York: Random House, Vintage Books, 1964.

Davis, James. *Presidential Primaries: Road to the White House.* New York: Thomas Y. Crowell, 1967.

Fenno, Richard F., Jr. *The President's Cabinet.* Cambridge, Mass.: Harvard University Press, 1959.

Frankel, Charles. *High on Foggy Bottom: An Outsider's Inside View of the Government.* New York: Harper & Row, Publishers, 1968.

Freeman, J. Leiper. *The Political Process: Executive Bureau-Legislative Committee Relations.* Revised edition. New York: Random House, 1965.

Fulbright, J.W. *The Pentagon Propaganda Machine.* New York: Liveright Publishing Corp., 1970.

Gawthrop, Louis C. *Bureaucratic Behavior in the Executive Branch.* New York: Free Press, 1969.

Larner, Jeremy. *Nobody Knows: Reflections on the McCarthy Campaign of 1968.* New York: Macmillan Co., 1970.

McCarthy, Eugene J. *The Year of the People.* New York: Doubleday & Co., 1969.

McGinniss, Joe. *The Selling of the President 1968.* New York: Trident Press, 1969.

Mendelsohn, Harold, and Crespi, Irving. *Polls, Television, and the New Politics.* Scranton: Chandler Publishing Co., 1970. *See esp.* pp. 264-314.

Pollard, James E. *The Presidents and the Press.* New York: Macmillan Co., 1947.

Polsby, Nelson W., and Wildavski, Aaron. *Presidential Elections.* Revised edition. New York: Charles Scribner's Sons, 1968.

Pomper, Gerald. *Nominating the President.* New York: W. W. Norton & Co., 1966.

Proxmire, William. *Report from Wasteland: America's Military-Industrial Complex.* New York: Frederick A. Praeger, 1970.

Reston, James. *The Artillery of the Press.* New York: Macmillan Co., 1966.

Rourke, Francis E. *Bureaucracy, Politics and Public Policy.* Boston: Little, Brown and Co., 1969.

Rubin, Bernard. *Political Television.* Belmont, Calif.; Wadsworth Publishing Co., 1967.

Schultze, Charles L.; Fried, Edward R.,; Rivlin, Alice M.; and Teeters, Nancy H. *Setting National Priorities: The 1971 Budget.* Washington, D.C.: Brookings Institution, 1970.

——. *Setting National Priorities: The 1972 Budget.* Washington, D.C.: Brookings Institution.

Sheehan, Neil, et al. *The Pentagon Papers.* New York: Bantam Books, 1971.

Sorensen, Theodore C. *Decision-Making in the White House.* Columbia University Press, 1963.

Stavis, Ben. *We Were the Campaign: New Hampshire to Chicago for McCarthy.* Boston: Beacon Press, 1969.

Warren, Sidney. *The President as World Leader.* Philadelphia: J. B. Lippincott Co., 1964.

White, Theodore H. *The Making of the President, 1960; The Making of the President, 1964; The Making of the President, 1968.* New York: Atheneum Publishers.

Witcover, Jules. *85 Days: The Last Campaign of Robert Kennedy.* New York: G. P. Putnam's Sons, 1969.

——. *The Resurrection of Richard Nixon.* New York: G. P. Putnam's Sons, 1970.

Yarmolinsky, Adam. *The Military Establishment: Its Impacts on American Society.* New York: Harper & Row Publishers, 1970.

IV. RECENT ARTICLES

Amlund, Curtis Arthur. "Executive-Legislative Imbalance: Truman to Kennedy." *Western Political Quarterly* 18 (September 1965): 640.

Baker Russell, and Peters, Charles. "The Prince and His Courtiers: At the White House, the Kremlin, and the Reich Chancellery." *Washington Monthly* 3 (March 1970): 34.

Barber, James D. "Analyzing Presidents: From Passive-Positive Taft to Active-Negative Nixon." *Washington Monthly* 1 (October 1969): 33.

Broder, David S. "Political Reporters in Presidential Politics." *Washington Monthly* 1 (February 1969): 20.

Brogan, Denis W. "The Highest Office." *American Heritage* August 1964, p. 5.

Carey, William D. "Presidential Staffing in the Sixties and Seventies." *Public Administration Review* 29 (September 1969): 450.

Cater, Douglass. "The Power of the President." *Center Magazine* 3 (1970): 69.

Commager, Henry Steele. "Can We Limit Presidential Power?" *New Republic,* 6 April 1968, p. 15.

Commager, Henry Steele. "The Misuse of Power." *New Republic,* 17 April 1971, p. 17.

Cronin, Thomas E. "Superman, Our Textbook President." *Washington Monthly* 2 (October 1970): 47.

Cunliffe, Marcus. "Defective Institution." *Commentary* 45 (February 1968): 27.

Donley, Richard, and Winter, David G. "Measuring the Motives of Public Officials at a Distance: An Explanatory Study of American Presidents." *Behavioral Science* 15 (May 1970): 227.

Edelman, Murray and Simon, Rita James. "Presidential Assassinations: Their Meaning and Impact on American Society." *Ethics* 79 (April 1969): 199.

Fenno, Richard F., Jr. "The Cabinet: Index to the Kennedy Way." *New York Times Magazine* 22 April 1962, p. 13.

Fox, Douglas M., and Clapp; Charles H. "The House Rules Committee and the Programs of the Kennedy and Johnson Administrations." *Midwest Journal of Political Science* 14 (November 1970): 667.

Greenstein, Fred I. "More on Children's Images of the President." *Public Opinion Quarterly* 25 (1961): 648.

———. "Popular Images of the President." *American Journal of Psychiatry* 122 (1965): 523.

Gustafson, Merlia. "The Religious Role of the President." *Midwest Journal of Political Science* 14 (November 1970): 708.

Hammond, Paul Y. "Presidents, Politics, and International Intervention." *Annals of the American Academy of Political and Social Science* 386 (November 1969): 10.

Harris, Richard E. "Annals of Politics: The Nomination of G. H. Carswell to the Court." *New Yorker,* 5 December 1970, p. 46; 12 December 1970, p. 53

Jacob, Charles E. "Limits of Presidential Leadership." *South Atlantic Quarterly* 62 (Autumn 1963): 461.

Kilpatrick, Carroll. "The Kennedy Style and Congress." *Virginia Quarterly Review* 39 (Winter 1963): 1.

Kotz, Nick. "Jamie Whitten, Permanent Secretary of Agriculture." *Washington Monthly.*

Long, Norton E. "Reflections on Presidential Power." *Public Administration Review* 29 (September 1969): 442.

Manley, John F. "Wilbur D. Mills: A Study in Congressional Influence." *American Political Science Review* 63 (June 1969): 442.

Mograth, C. Peter. "Lyndon Johnson and the Paradox of the Presidency." *Yale Review* 54 (June 1965): 481.

Moyers, Bill, and Sidey, Hugh. "The White House Staff vs. the Cabinet." *Washington Monthly* 1 (February, 1969): 2.

Moynihan, Daniel P. "The Presidency & the Press." *Commentary* 51 (March 1971): 41.

Mueller, John E. "Presidential Popularity from Truman to Johnson." *American Political Science Review* 64 (March 1970): 18.

Neustadt, Richard E. "Approaches to Staffing the Presidency: Notes on FDR and JFK." *American Political Science Review* 57 (December 1963): 855.

———. "Kennedy in the Presidency: A Premature Appraisal." *Political Science Quarterly* 79 (September 1964): 321.

Pincus, Walter. "After the Pentagon Papers—The Same Old Story." *New York,* 16 August 1971, p. 46.

Pipe, G. Russell. "Congressional Liaison: The Executive Branch Consolidates its Relations with Congress." *Public Administration* 26 (March 1966): 14.

Polsby, Nelson W.; Gallaher, Miriam; and Rundquist, Barry Spencer. "The Growth of the Seniority System in the United States House of Representatives." *American Political Science Review* 63 (September 1969): 787.

Reveley, W. Taylor III. "Presidential War-Making: Constitutional Prerogative or Usurpation?" *Virginia Law Review* 55 (November 1969): 1243.

Rothchild, John. "Cooling Down the War: The Senate's Lame Doves." *Washington Monthly* 3 (August, 1971): 6.

Schlesinger, Arthur M. Jr. "Limits and Excesses of Presidential Power." *Saturday Review,* 3 May 1969, p. 17.

Sullivan, Robert R. "The Role of the Presidency in Shaping Lower Level Policy-Making Processes." *Polity* 3 (Winter 1970): 201.

Symington, Stuart. "Congress' Right to Know: Withholding of Military Information by the Executive Branch." *New York Times Magazine* 9 August 1970, p. 7.

Thomas, Norman C., and Wolman, Harold L. "The Presidency and Policy Formulation: The Task Force Device." *Public Administration Review* 29 (September 1969): 459.

Vile, M. J. C. "The Formation and Execution of Policy in the United States." *Political Quarterly* 33 (April 1962): 162.

Wicker, Tom. "The Presidency Under Scrutiny." *Harper's,* October 1969, p. 92.